"What a privilege to be asked to endorse a book by Avery Willis! This is a man who has been so greatly used by God to help others fulfill the Great Commission in discipling others. You'll find yourself not only blessed by his book but also eager to put its words into practice."

— KAY ARTHUR, cofounder, Precept Ministries International

"If you want to be mentored in how to live in the presence of the Lord, *Learning to Soar* gives you the GPS settings to get there. Avery and Matt Willis make a great contribution to the body of Christ by sharing their lives with transparency and reality. Get it, read it, and pass it on to your friends."

— LAUREN LIBBY, president, Trans World Radio

"Avery Willis, a leading missionary statesman worldwide, has joined together with his grandson Matt, who is a part of this exciting new generation now emerging. The combination of generations, like a Paul and a Timothy, an Elijah and Elisha, will have the greatest impact the world has seen to date in completing the great commission. *Learning to Soar* will prepare you through the eyes of the visionary zeal of youth and the seasoned experience and wisdom of a senior leader to find your place in fulfilling your destiny and God's dream for transforming the world."

— LOREN CUNNINGHAM, founder, Youth With A Mission; president, University of the Nations

"Avery Willis is a man with a lot of experience. He has provided excellent input to many people through the years. One thing I particularly like about him is his joyful faith. He has indeed 'learned to soar.'"

— STEVE DOUGLASS, president, Campus Crusade for Christ International

"It was with great joy that I received Avery and his grandson Matt's book *Learning to Soar*. It is a timely and necessary publication that will encourage all believers to face the challenges and changes of this world with greater courage and certainty. I am certain that many will be blessed and strengthened by the practical and inspiring teaching contained in its pages."

— GRAHAM POWER, founder, Global Day of Prayer and Unashamedly Ethical; chairman, Power Group

"It thrills me when one of my personal heroes decides to write on a subject that depicts his journey. Avery Willis knows the God of victories, who grows us in the midst of our trials. As you read this volume, note how His purposes are becoming a reality in your own life. A much-needed book at this time in history."

— DR. JOHNNY HUNT, president, Southern Baptist Convention; pastor, Woodstock Baptist Church, Woodstock, Georgia

"Avery Willis is a gifted communicator of biblical truth to all ages and cultures, and we were privileged to have him as a guest on our TV broadcast. This unique new book, written with his grandson, thoughtfully employs powerful word pictures to weave relevant scriptural concepts into our personal lives. A must-read for those whose 'nests' are being stirred!"
—RON AND ANN MAINSE, president, Crossroads Christian Communications, hosts of *100 Huntley Street*

"Avery Willis always challenges us to raise our view of God and our expectation of Him working in our lives. His newest work, *Learning to Soar*, will challenge you to raise your spiritual life to a higher level."
—RONNIE FLOYD, pastor, First Baptist Church, Springdale, Arkansas, and Pinnacle Hills Church, Rogers, Arkansas

"Let's face it: Transitions can be tough. Avery Willis and Matt Willis provide wonderful insight into facing these transitions and challenges. Using the imagery of the eagle as presented in Scripture, Avery provides valuable wisdom backed up by decades of experience, while Matt writes with the zeal and perspective of a young man and husband at the beginning of a lifelong journey of service to God. You will find this book helpful no matter your phase of life."
—DAVID WESLEY WHITLOCK, president, Oklahoma Baptist University

"When God stirs your nest, it is often in relation to what He wants to accomplish through you for His purposes. This book by Avery and Matt Willis will help you discern God's voice in the midst of living life. There is no greater satisfaction than being aligned with what God is doing, and I believe God will use this book to help you understand what He wants to do in and through you."
—BOB CRESON, president/CEO, Wycliffe Bible Translators USA

"Avery and Matt Willis have given us a wonderful study in trusting God in the uncertainties and trials of life. *Learning to Soar* provides lessons on how God uses the circumstances of life to help us mature and grow in Him, enabling us to soar above those situations that drag us down and cause us to doubt the unconditional love of our Father. I recommend this book to anyone desiring to learn God's ways, spread their wings, and soar in their walk with Him."
—PAUL SABER, chief operating officer, Billy Graham Evangelistic Association

"Avery is a great storyteller, and in this book he powerfully tells the story of the eagle and how God has used this analogy to explain how we are to become. As I read the book, I remembered how God had worked in my life and family and the challenge to trust God in the future."
—MORGAN JACKSON, international director, Faith Comes By Hearing

"This book is personally engaging from beginning to end! It contains the truths we need to hear from Scripture and from God's nature written into His creation. Avery and Matt have given us all an encouraging guidebook for troubled times."

—DR. JOEL C. HUNTER, senior pastor, Northland–A Church Distributed, Orlando, Florida

"What is the difference in those who are able to deal with life's hard times and those who aren't? Much of the victory is found in understanding four ways that God works. In *Learning to Soar,* you can learn these four ways and move toward a new level of victorious Christian living, beginning today!"

—DR. BOBBY H. WELCH, strategist for global evangelical relations, Southern Baptist Convention

"What a joy to recommend Avery's new book. His leadership, writings, teaching, and training have influenced millions of believers in countries around the world. Having known him and watched him up close, I can testify that he humbly lives what he teaches. May the Lord cause readers to become restless to get out of the nest and fly!"

—MARTIN DEACON, vice president, call2all

"Avery Willis is a man of great conviction, passion, and vision. I am thankful to God for him, and I am thankful for the example he, along with his grandson Matt, are setting for us. In this book, they share from the heart and encourage us all."

—ALBERT R. MOHLER JR., president, The Southern Baptist Theological Seminary (SBC), Louisville, Kentucky

"Using the well-researched life development of an eagle, Avery Willis brings to life parallels between the development of an eagle's life and the development of the believer's life. This insightful account will both equip you for advancing in the discipleship process and inspire you to pursue the abundant life that God has for all who follow Him."

—JIM AUSTIN, executive director and treasurer, South Carolina Baptist Convention

"All my research into personal discipleship and the condition of the church in America today points to the need for *Learning to Soar* for individuals, churches, and the nation. Avery and Matt Willis have done us a service by applying to us today the pertinent message that God gave first to Moses and Israel. If you want to experience personal renewal and see spiritual awakening among God's people, don't miss this book."

—ED STETZER, president, LifeWay Research

"Avery Willis is a man who cares first and foremost about seeing the world come to know Jesus. He knows this happens best when we make disciples rather than converts. This book will help new believers understand how God works as He shapes and matures them, and it will introduce mature Christians to a methodology (biblical storytelling) that Jesus used to make the truth relatable in the lives of His disciples."

—JIM PUTMAN, author, *Church is a Team Sport*, international speaker, senior pastor, Real Life Ministries, Post Falls, Idaho

"*Learning to Soar* is an important book for those dealing with the adversity that accompanies difficult times. Avery Willis masterfully uses the analogy of an eagle's development to illustrate how God often uses dire situations to bring His people to unimaginable heights. This book is an excellent resource to help Christians find God's will through troubled times and factor Him into their lives and their decision making."

—DAVID "MAC" MCQUISTON, president/CEO, The CEO Forum

"Weaving together powerful cross-generational life examples and clear biblical truth, Avery and Matt Willis have unpacked the rich metaphor of the eagle as a pattern of God's dealing with His children. Both practical and inspiring, *Learning to Soar* will give you fresh perspective on God's ways and renewed passion to pursue everything He has planned for your life."

—STEVE MOORE, president/CEO, The Mission Exchange (formerly EFMA)

"Mr. Willis, the book that you wrote with your grandson is absolutely fantastic! *Learning to Soar* has brought SO much out of me that it's like I now know myself—me—better than ever before. Thank you for writing this book!"

—LINNE DEACON, age twelve

"Avery and Matt Willis have given the church an incredible gift. At a time when so many young people want to be mentored by elders and when our churches desperately need excellent materials to grow the next generation of leaders, this book serves as a source of encouragement to take that next courageous step of faith and trust God."

—ROY PETERSON, president/CEO, The Seed Company (an affiliate of Wycliffe Bible Translators)

"Avery Willis and his grandson, Matt, have collaborated on an inspirational book that will challenge every reader to a new dimension of experiencing the power and fullness of God."

—JERRY RANKIN, president, International Mission Board, Southern Baptist Convention

AVERY T. WILLIS JR.

AND

MATT WILLIS

LEARNING TO
SOAR

How to Grow Through Transitions and Trials

NAVPRESS

Navpress is the publishing ministry of The Navigators, an international Christian organization and leader in personal spiritual development. NavPress is committed to helping people grow spiritually and enjoy lives of meaning and hope through personal and group resources that are biblically rooted, culturally relevant, and highly practical.

For a free catalog go to www.navpress.com
or call 1.800.366.7788 in the United States or 1.800.839.4769 in Canada.

© 2009 by Avery T. Willis Jr. and Matt Willis

All rights reserved. No part of this publication may be reproduced in any form without written permission from NavPress, P.O. Box 35001, Colorado Springs, CO 80935. www.navpress.com

NAVPRESS and the NAVPRESS logo are registered trademarks of NavPress. Absence of ® in connection with marks of NavPress or other parties does not indicate an absence of registration of those marks.

ISBN: 978-1-60006-697-9

Cover design by Arvid Wallen
Cover image by Shutterstock

Published in association with the literary agency of Sanford Communications, Inc., Portland, Oregon, www.sanfordci.com.

Some of the anecdotal illustrations in this book are true to life and are included with the permission of the persons involved. All other illustrations are composites of real situations, and any resemblance to people living or dead is coincidental.

Unless otherwise identified, all Scripture quotations in this publication are taken from the *Holy Bible, New International Version*® (NIV®). Copyright © 1973, 1978, 1984 by International Bible Society. Used by permission of Zondervan. All rights reserved. Other versions used include: the New American Standard Bible® (NASB), Copyright © 1960, 1962, 1963, 1968, 1971, 1972, 1973, 1975, 1977, 1995 by The Lockman Foundation. Used by permission; the New King James Version (NKJV). Copyright © 1982 by Thomas Nelson, Inc. Used by permission. All rights reserved; the King James Version (KJV); *THE MESSAGE* (MSG). Copyright © 1993, 1994, 1995, 1996, 2000, 2001, 2002. Used by permission of NavPress Publishing Group; and The International Standard Version, Copyright © 1994-2009 by the ISV Foundation. All rights reserved internationally.

Library of Congress Cataloging-in-Publication Data

Willis, Avery T.
   Learning to soar : how to grow through transitions and trials / Avery T. Willis, Jr., Matt Willis.
      p. cm.
   Includes bibliographical references.
   ISBN 978-1-60006-697-9
   1. Spiritual formation. I. Willis, Matt, 1983- II. Title.
   BV4511.W55 2009
   248.4--dc22
                              2009008121

Printed in the United States of America

3 4 5 6 7 8 / 13 12 11 10 09

I, Avery, dedicate this book to my sixteen grandchildren—Matt Willis,

Kyle Willis, Kara Willis, Stephanie Brown, Kristine Brown, Lauren

Brown, Kent Willis, Thomas Willis, Hannah Willis, Amy Willis, Amber

McAtee, Mikayla McAtee, Connor McAtee, Kenna Willis, Kayla Willis,

and Carver Willis—with the prayer that they will all continue to follow

Jesus and to teach their children to walk in truth (Isaiah 59:21).

I, Matt, dedicate this book to my best friend and wife, Allison.

CONTENTS

FOREWORD

In the book you now hold, my good friend Avery Willis and his twenty-something grandson Matt offer a fascinating look at four ways God guides you through the process of understanding and living out His purpose for your life.

God Himself describes in Deuteronomy 32:11 the process that He uses to develop your faith and character so you can carry out His purpose. Two easy-to-understand analogies—eagles and the real-life laboratory of Israel's journey from Egypt to the Promised Land—teach how He leads His people. As God compares Himself to a parent eagle, He tells us that as the eagle guides the development of its offspring so He develops His people.

One of the most fascinating parallels is how, when the mother eagle knows it's time for her growing eaglets to leave the nest, she stirs the nest with her talons in order to make the nest less comfortable. As the fluffy down feathers of the birth nest are scraped away, the exposed twigs underneath now stick the growing eaglet, and the discomfort motivates him to leave the security nest and test his wings. Over time, the eaglet ventures farther and higher and eventually learns to soar—but he would never have taken the first step had he not experienced the relative discomfort of the nest in transition.

The ways of the eagle beautifully illustrate God's nurture and purpose for His people—not only for the Israelites on their journey to the Promised Land but also for you and me, today, as we encounter the challenges of contemporary life. You will discover anew just how great, how magnificent, are God's ways for you. You'll marvel at how He loves you so much that He nurtures you with care, using the transitions and trials of life to help you grow stronger in Christian maturity. As you and I journey in faith toward spiritual adulthood, God wants to give us "wings like eagles" (Isaiah 40:31) so that we may truly soar to new heights in living out our God-ordained purpose.

You are in for a God experience. I urge you to take the time to go through the time-proven processes that God uses to help us know and do His will and learn to soar by the power of the Spirit. It's a God thing!

—RICK WARREN
Pastor, Saddleback Church

PREFACE

No one needs to alert us that these times in our nation and the world are the most demanding we've known in many years. The twenty-first century has ushered in very difficult transitions and trials that continue to challenge all of us. What are we facing, and how should we respond?

Certainly, one of the greatest fears in the hearts of many is the rise of global terrorism. All of us in America were greatly affected by 9/11, and terrorism continues to be a major threat worldwide. Daily we're bombarded by tragic news coming out of Iraq, Afghanistan, and other parts of the world. And we wonder, *What's next for our own nation?*

We've also experienced a great moral, ethical, and spiritual decline in recent decades that permeates not only our culture but also our Christian community. Political and corporate scandals are all too common at all levels. Sexual promiscuity, pornography, and abortion plague the nation — even among evangelicals. And it is shocking to know that divorce is nearly as prevalent among Christians as non-Christians. The trauma in our families is devastating and the fallout unknown for future generations.

Economic crisis continues to affect us all. Retirement and college savings have dwindled due to uncertain markets. Well-meaning individuals and families have lost jobs and homes while companies large and small have declared bankruptcy.

In short, we live in dark and uncertain times.

Learning to Soar, written by my friend Avery Willis and his grandson Matt, will both encourage you and challenge you to live a life of purpose and mission in the midst of strife. Every Christian's life is designed by God to be "light" in the darkness and "salt" to bring out flavor and meaning in a fearful, uncertain world. As you read, you'll learn to live your life abundantly before a watching, hurting world.

It is Christ's presence in our lives that demonstrates both to ourselves and to those around us the difference He truly makes in difficult times. In Christ alone our faith is strengthened. When the storms rage He will remind you, "Be of good cheer! It is I; do not be afraid" (Matthew 14:27, NKJV). Only then can you grow in Him through the rough transitions and trials of life. And it is then that you will model the peace of Christ in the lives of others.

—HENRY BLACKABY
Author of *Experiencing God*

A Note from the Authors

Your authors have a special relationship. Not only is Matt Willis the first grandson of Avery Willis, but Matt also preached his first Sunday sermon exactly fifty years after his granddad's first sermon! The timing was not intentional and was discovered afterward.

Matt is also following in his granddad's missionary steps. He accompanied Avery to Cuba while still in high school and has participated in a total of ten missions trips to nine countries. He directed the Avery T. Willis Center for Global Outreach at Oklahoma Baptist University, where both of them graduated. Currently, Matt and his family are serving in Asia.

This book is a true coauthorship. Because we don't like the awkwardness of switching back and forth from one author to another, the book uses first-person singular from Avery's perspective. Matt wrote the sidebars, which distinguish the uniqueness of Avery's seasoned wisdom compared with Matt's midtwenties perspective. Note also that we have used real names (first and last) in every case that we were able to obtain permission to do so. When only a first name is used, the story is still true, but the name is usually a pseudonym because that person currently lives in a dangerous place.

ACKNOWLEDGMENTS

We both thank our families for letting us write this book in spite of all the other responsibilities we had going on. Thank you to family and friends who read through our manuscript, offered critiques, and lent us stories: Brandon Shafer, Dustin Sarver, Joshua Greever, and many others. Special thanks to Allison, Matt's wife; Sherrie Brown, Avery's first daughter; and Sherrie's daughter Stephanie Brown, who all helped in editing it. Thank you to David Sanford, Rebekah Clark, and Elizabeth Jones for serving us and helping this work serve more people. We appreciate Dan Benson, Mike Miller, Jessica Chappell, and others at NavPress who enabled this book to take wing. Thanks to all of you who have helped us make this book possible.

I, Matt, thank Allison for sharing some of my responsibilities so that I could coauthor this book, encouraging me, listening to me, and unconditionally loving me. Thank you, Joshua and Jenna, for enriching my life as my sweet kids. Thank you to my high-school English teachers, Lajuana Moore and Marsha Scott, who told me I had a talent for writing and helped me refine it. Thank you to Randy, Denyce, Kyle, Megan, and Kara for loving and influencing me. Thank you, Granddad, for asking me to write this with you; it has been my joy and honor. Most of all, I thank God for making me, saving me, equipping me, and calling me to You, beyond the natural.

I, Avery, thank countless friends who have encouraged me to put these truths in print. Thank you to many who have given suggestions for making it real to people in all kinds of situations. Thank you to the many prayer partners who prayed for us as we wrote and sought the best publisher. I especially thank Matt for the privilege of writing this together. Through his research on eagles, he has insisted on an accurate portrayal of this growth process. What a privilege it has been to share these ways of God together and to watch Matt put them into action.

INTRODUCTION

There is a reason the writers of the Old Testament used eagles in their metaphors. Magnificent and fierce, these large birds were a symbol of strength and boldness and an inspiration to the prophets who watched them from below. If you understand and apply the stories of eagles and the Israelites to your own life, you will gain new insight into God's ways because God frequently chose to reveal Himself through both of them—and told Moses to sing and write about them—for our benefit. And understanding God's ways helps us truly know Him and live in closer communion with Him.

Israel's story dominates the Old Testament and is a most telling demonstration of how God works. The eagle's story is woven throughout the story of Israel and is found most explicitly in Deuteronomy 32:11-12. It is our hope that you will be inspired by these twin threads—eagles and Israel—to look more closely at how God pushes you to grow and triumph through transitions and trials.

- In part 1 you will learn how God uses hardships to move you from where you are to the place where you are willing to change and align with His purposes.
- In part 2 you will learn to have patience in the presence of God and to exercise faith in trouble while God is working out His plan for you.
- In part 3 you will learn how to put faith into action as God teaches you through trial and error.
- In part 4 you will learn how to fulfill your God-given potential as you operate in the power of His Spirit.

An eagle grows from birth to maturity as a process; the transition does not happen overnight. Likewise, your spiritual growth is a lifelong journey that will probably not look like one straight line. With that in mind, here is a diagram of the process that eagles, Israel, and you may go through on the way to learning to soar. This model summarizes the book and will occasionally be referenced.

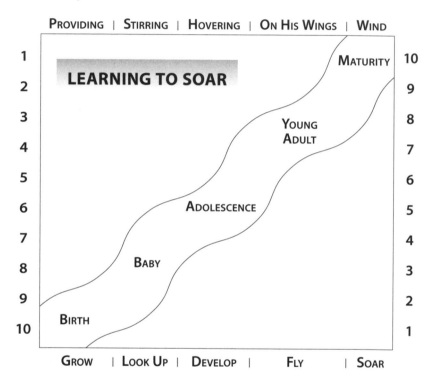

You will notice that the up-and-down path in the middle of the diagram follows the growth of the eagle. The captions above the diagram show what the parent eagle is doing at each stage. The captions underneath show what the eagle is experiencing. The numbers on the left side of the chart show the decreasing degree of the parent's responsibility. It begins with a 10 — full responsibility — and moves to a 1. The eagle's responsibility grows as the parent's decreases.

This diagram also mirrors how God led Israel and how He leads us as His disciples. God took Israel on this same journey, and He uses this same pattern to help us grow and learn to soar. As you read the book, use this diagram as a road map to your growth to see where you are and where you need to go. Although the graph pictures the full development of the whole person, it can also be applied to a specific trait, characteristic, or growth area. We can be generally mature yet have one facet of our lives still stuck at the child stage.

Finally, keep a pen and journal with you as you delve into this book. Allow time to meditate upon the questions at the end of each chapter. Write down your answers and your own questions so that you will fully experience this book's insights. I have kept a journal like this for years. Each morning I read a chapter or so in the Bible and record what God said to me. Then I write down what I said to God. Each month or so I read back through my journal. I am always amazed at what I wrote. Often I discover that God has been saying the same thing to me for weeks, and I am just waking up to it! Try it with this book—take the time to answer the questions after each chapter and see what God has done and is doing in your life.

To get the maximum benefit from this book, join a small group that discusses a chapter a week and tells Bible stories from Israel's experience. The Discussion Guide for Small Groups beginning on page 143 provides guidance to the leader and the storyteller. Go to www.learningtosoar.org to see demonstrations of how to tell a Bible story effectively and ask questions that will get every member into the Bible and the Bible into their lives. You will experience the Bible in a distinctively new way. Most life changes come in relationships. A small group will give you support, challenge you, and help you fulfill your commitments to Christ. It is a fun way to follow Christ and learn to soar together.

PART ONE

GOD STIRS
YOUR NEST

Like an eagle that stirs up its nest,
That hovers over its young,
He spread His wings and caught them,
He carried them on His pinions.
The LORD *alone guided him,*
And there was no foreign god with him.

— DEUTERONOMY 32:11-12, NASB

CHAPTER I

STIRRING THE NEST

Like an eagle that stirs up its nest . . .
The LORD alone guided him.
— DEUTERONOMY 32:11-12, NASB

The baby eagle perches on the side of the rough nest, digs in his talons, and faces his parent. The parent eagle claws out the soft lining of the nest, thus exposing the jagged bones, sticks, and briars of their home. The eaglet arches his head back in shock as if to ask, *What are you doing?* He tries to stop his parent, but he is no match. Realizing his weakness, he waddles to the last little spot of soft leaves and feathers left in the nest, but the parent plucks that out as well.

Now everywhere the baby eagle turns, he gets stuck. He cannot sit or lie down without causing even more pain. All he can do is cry and wonder, *Why are you doing this to me?*[1]

The parent eagle knows that its offspring were not born to stay in a soft nest. Eaglets need to mature and learn how to fly like the majestic animals they were born to be. The parents must give the eaglets a reason to leave or else they would want to stay there forever. Yet reluctant and unaware, the eaglets are confused at their parents' actions.

Do you ever feel like the baby eagle? Have unpleasant changes caused you to question why something has happened to you? You may have wondered whether the difficulties were caused by unfortunate circumstances, Satan, or even your own incompetence. But have you considered that God may be causing the difficulties you are facing? If so, you may be thinking (as I have many times), *Lord, I don't know what You are doing, but I sense that You want to do something new in my life.* God often brings difficult circumstances into our lives in order to prompt us away from complacency and a spiritual plateau.

A nest is a blessing from God. Living in a nest means that you belong to someone. It's a place where you're wanted, you're secure, and it just feels right. God built an amazing nest for me before I was even born. That nest included a godly heritage, part of which is due to Avery, my granddad and the coauthor of this book. I greatly respect him, for he knows and soars in God's ways. (God's ways are His methods. They encompass God's acts, which are His single moves.) I love to hear God's ways from Avery because I'm young and tend to recognize only God's acts. A nest is a great experience because its youthful inhabitants aren't yet wise enough to see God's ways. That's why God's actions, such as His stirring, can be so confusing to us in the nest.

This is a story of eagles, of Israel, and ultimately of God. You should find yourself in the story. God has provided a real-life example (Israel) of how to respond to Him, and He gives us the eagle's story to help us remember the ways He works with His people. Through this process you will learn how God works—even in the midst of hardship—to give you direction and comfort as you discover that His purposes are always for your good and His glory.

The Bible employs the analogy of the eagle twenty-five times in the Old and New Testaments to help God's people understand His ways. God shows us His ways in a detailed account of how He led His people out of bondage, found in the books of Exodus, Leviticus, Numbers, Deuteronomy, and Joshua. In them, God compares His ways to the ways of eagles. After God delivered Israel out of slavery in Egypt, He told them, "You yourselves have seen what I did to Egypt, and how I carried you on eagles' wings and brought you to myself" (Exodus 19:4).

Forty years later, God told Moses to teach the Israelites a song recounting the story of their deliverance so that they would remember God's ways. In the song, Moses pictured the Lord as a fine eagle:

Like an eagle that stirs up its nest,
That hovers over its young,
He spread His wings and caught them,
He carried them on His pinions.
The LORD alone guided him,
And there was no foreign god with him. (Deuteronomy 32:11-12,
NASB)

Years later, the psalmist David wrote, "[God] made known his ways to Moses, his deeds to the people of Israel" (Psalm 103:7). Anyone can see the *actions* of God, but He wants you to know His *ways*. It took only a brief time for the Israelites to recognize God's mighty *actions* when He led them out of Egypt with ten astonishing plagues. However, God revealed His *ways* to Moses through eighty years of intimate fellowship. Once we understand God's actions in light of His ways, then we can better know Him and grow in Him through obedience. God's ways have not changed since He clarified them in the Bible, and He wants to help you better understand His ways so that you will not only walk with Him but also soar with Him on wings like eagles (see Isaiah 40:31). If you don't know God's ways, you can misunderstand His actions, as the Israelites and the baby eagle did.

In the Bible, God Himself tells us there's much we can learn about His ways and about how to become Christlike disciples by understanding the ways of eagles. Let's begin at the eagle's nest to explain why God stirs our nests.

A SECURE NEST

An eagle's nest is an impressive structure. The bald eagle, America's national emblem, builds larger nests than any other bird in the world. The largest eagle's nest, found in Florida, was twenty feet deep, nine and a half feet wide, and weighed almost three tons![2] Some nests are strong enough to hold an adult human being. Mates for life, pairs of eagles build their nests high on a safe ledge or in a tall tree, away from the dangers of predators. They use sticks, branches, and bones to create the nest and then line it with leaves, fur, and other soft material to create an area to cradle their eggs. (Each spring, the eagles come back to their nests and line them again.) The nest provides both comfort and security to the offspring in the weeks before they are able to fly.

Baby eagles have it made — the presence and care of their parents is constant and unchanging. From the moment the female lays her eggs, the parent eagles cover them by pressing the warmest part of their bellies against the eggs, providing incubation until they are hatched.[3] Once the eaglets hatch, their mother engulfs them beneath her wings nearly twenty-four hours a day for the first month of their lives. In the rain, those wings become an umbrella; they provide shade from the heat, a blanket in the cold. If a predator comes near, the mother eagle vigorously defends her young ones. Up to eight times a day, the male eagle brings the meat of its prey to the female, who feeds it to her babies. All they do is open their mouths and accept the nourishment.[4] Isolated from the chaos of the world around them, the eaglets have nothing to fear. They can't comprehend any reason why life should not remain that way forever.

It's never the parents' intention, however, for the nest to become their young ones' perpetual home.

ALL SHOOK UP

If the eaglet could see through its parents' eyes, it would know that this infant stage of life cannot continue indefinitely. The time comes to encourage the young ones to mature — literally, to stir the nest. The parents do this by clawing out the leaves, fur, and other soft materials, exposing the briars, sticks, and bones. What had been a comfortable home is now a bed of thorns.

Once eaglets become uncomfortable in the stirred nest, they are more willing to leave it — yet they may still need more prodding. Hunger usually works. The male eagle stops bringing meat to his mate to feed their offspring, who sometimes have grown too heavy to fly just before it's time for them to learn. What appears to be an attempt by the parents to starve the eaglets is actually a way to prepare them to leave the nest and find their own food.

If the hungry eaglets are able to fly yet still remain in the nest, their parents tempt them to leave the nest for their next meal. The male eagle may swoop past the nest with a delectable jackrabbit or fish in its talons. As it passes, the hungry eaglets stand at the edge of the nest, shrieking for the food. The eagle may continually fly by, just out of reach. Sometimes, in their eagerness for a morsel, the eaglets climb to the edge of the nest and lose their balance, but the parent eagle flies away and drops the food a distance from the nest where the eaglets can see it but not reach it.[5] At times the parent eagle will even beat them with her wings to get them to leave the nest.

The eaglets are confused. First, their once comfortable nest jabs and stings, and then there's nothing to eat. Even their own parents, it seems, have turned against them. That's not the case, however; the eaglets' wise parents are not stifling their growth but rather taking it to the next level.

Deuteronomy 32:11 says God develops us like "an eagle that *stirs* up its nest" (emphasis mine). The original Hebrew word for *stir* primarily means "to open or bare."[6] The Hebrew word used here means "to open one's eyes, to wake up, to lift up, to be made naked, or to stir up." When God stirs your nest, He makes the nest naked. He reaches the core of who you are, and nothing is hidden from Him. No mask you wear fools God. What lies in your heart that you don't wish God to expose? A secret sin? Unresolved conflict with a person? Your doubt? Your fears? A selfish dream?

God stirred the nest — *really* stirred the nest — of one of my roommates from college, Brandon Shafer. Brandon was a seminary student in New Orleans and had left town to visit friends for the weekend when he learned that Hurricane Katrina would hit the city.

"The sick feeling of despair swept over me as I watched television reports over the next few days describe the devastation to almost everything in the city," he said. "I had lived in a first-floor apartment, and after seeing several different pictures of my apartment complex, I realized that anything I had left behind was more than likely a 100 percent loss. Not only did I lose material possessions, but I also lost my school and my job."

God displayed His power to Brandon by providing him with food, lodging, and friends. God even gave him a youth-ministry position in Lake Charles, Louisiana. Brandon realized that God used Hurricane Katrina to help him grow more in his relationship with God than he ever had in such a short period of time.

GOD'S WORK AMONG THE ISRAELITES

The story of an eagle stirring its nest resonated clearly with the Israelites in the wilderness, for they had recently experienced a similar situation. The nation of Israel began with the family of Abraham, to whom God promised He would make a great nation through his son. God multiplied the descendants of Abraham in the nest of Canaan through Isaac and Isaac's son Jacob, whom God later named Israel. Israel's son Joseph was taken to Egypt as a slave but eventually became the pharaoh's second-in-command.

At that time, a famine was occurring among Abraham's descendants in Canaan, so Pharaoh invited Joseph's relatives to come and live in the land of Goshen, the best property available in Egypt. God used a famine to get the people of Israel to leave their adopted country and go to Goshen, just as an eagle uses hunger to entice its young out of their nest. Goshen was a fabulous nest where Israel's family was well fed, fruitful, and increased greatly in number. Life was good for the Israelites, and they assumed it would stay that way.

Four hundred years later, however, God stirred Israel's nest a second time when a new pharaoh enslaved the Israelites because he feared they would outnumber and overpower his people, the Egyptians. He made their lives "bitter with hard labor" as they built the storage cities of Pithom and Rameses (Exodus 1:14). The more he oppressed them, the more they multiplied; the more they multiplied, the more he oppressed them. The Israelites' world quickly turned from one of comfort to one of chaos.

Where was God? Was He missing this? This was the nation He promised to create and bless so the whole world would be blessed. Had He abandoned them?

Quite the contrary. God was not blind to what His people were experiencing. This "stirring" was part of His plan to bless His people—and through them to bless all the peoples of the earth. In His sovereignty, God was fulfilling His promise made to Abraham in Genesis 15:13-14:

> Then the LORD said to him, "Know for certain that your descendants will be strangers in a country not their own, and they will

be enslaved and mistreated four hundred years. But I will punish the nation they serve as slaves, and afterward they will come out with great possessions."

God took away the Israelites' comfort so that they would be willing to leave Egypt, go to the Promised Land, and become the people He had called them to be.

God spoke to Israel through a later part of Moses' song: "I have wounded and I will heal" (Deuteronomy 32:39). God exposed Israel to the thorny parts of the nest because the people would have been unwilling to leave its comfort to fulfill His destiny for them. Sure enough, when God removed their comfortable surroundings, Israel cried out for deliverance, just as baby eagles do.

GOD'S WORK IN US

God often stirs our nests to get us off our own agenda and onto His—even though we don't understand what is happening or why. Why not ask God what the new circumstances, open doors, or challenging opportunities you are facing have to do with His purpose for your life? As a nation, Israel could not be conformed to God's plan and stay in Egypt; they had to leave Egypt to be able to go to the Promised Land. Likewise, we cannot grow up to soar as eagles if we insist on staying in the secure nest.

God stirred my nest when I was a freshman in college. I had spent the first semester having a good time. For the first time in my life I was responsible for my own decisions without my parents telling me what to do. God began to speak to me about the irresponsible way I was living and the role He had for me.

"You are a nominal Christian," He said.

"But, Lord," I said, "I am doing everything my church has asked me to do. I attend Sunday school, worship services twice on Sunday, church-training classes, and even prayer meetings on Wednesday night. I tithe and even help around the church."

"You are a nominal Christian," He said. "You are not a disciple who denies himself, takes up his cross daily, and follows me" (see Luke 9:23).

Although I was disturbed, I knew He was right. He kept pushing me to surrender my life to Him. I waffled. I knew I was at a crossroads. I sensed that I would make a decision either to become a true disciple of Christ or to be a mediocre Christian for the rest of my life.

God reminded me of D. L. Moody, who heard Henry Varley say, "It remains to be seen what God will do with a man who gives himself up wholly to Him." Moody responded by saying, "Well, I will be that man."[7] No doubt he did that, because armed with only a third-grade education, he led hundreds of thousands to Christ in the United States and England — not to mention establishing Moody Bible Institute and Moody Press.

I told God that I was not a leader and that I could not do what He was asking me to do. He showed me the scripture, "For the eyes of the Lord move to and fro throughout the earth that He may strongly support those whose heart is completely His" (2 Chronicles 16:9, NASB). God showed me that He is looking all over the world for someone — anyone — who will love Him with all his or her heart, soul, and strength and will obediently do whatever He asks. When God finds a person like that, He demonstrates His strength to and through him or her. I said, "Lord, I am such an ordinary person that if You do anything with my life, everyone will know that You did it." I committed myself to be a disciple, deny myself, take up my cross daily, and follow Him. That decision changed the course of my life as I responded positively to God's stirring.

What kind of disciple are you? You are not automatically a mature disciple just because you are a Christian. Have you really surrendered all to Christ? Even if you once made that decision, are you continuing to grow as His disciple? "'Come, follow me,' Jesus said, 'and I will make you fishers of men'" (Matthew 4:19). Discipleship is a lifelong process of following Jesus, becoming like Him, and carrying on His mission. Jesus invites you into the thrilling adventure of maturing as a disciple and making disciples.

Is God stirring your nest to help you follow Him? Do you need to grow in Christ, launch out on a new adventure, or make a significant life change? God never leaves us in our comfortable surroundings. He makes a habit of stirring us up to do His will.

What is your story? Are you confused at what God is doing in your life? Don't worry; God has provided a real-life example of how to respond to Him through Israel's experience, and He gives us the eagle's story to help us remember the ways He works with His people.

When I was growing up, one of my nests was attending Christian schools. As a freshman in high school, I grew discontented because all of my schoolmates either were Christians or did a good job pretending. Even though many of them were good people, I had trouble connecting with them on a personal or spiritual level.

One night I cried so hard in prayer, asking that God provide me with close friends and witnessing opportunities. He stirred up my loneliness first to draw me deeper to Him and then to prepare me for a transition in my relationships and routine. God stirred my nest and called me to transfer to a public school, where He gave me opportunities to make a lot of friends and introduce some of them to Christ. Instead of having fifty private-school classmates who all grew up in church, I graduated from a public high school with a thousand people from all types of backgrounds and with all sorts of needs. I am thankful for the Christian education that prepared me to be a light for Christ, but that nest was designed to be my launching pad rather than my permanent abode.

As new believers, we feel secure inside God's nest—as we should —because when He makes us one of His children, He does everything to protect and nurture our growth so we may become more like Him. But in time, for that same reason, God removes the lining from our nests. The following circumstances in our lives may be a sign of God's stirring:

- Job changes
- Relationship problems
- Feelings of discontentment
- Unforeseen events
- New desires

WRESTLING WITH GOD

Maybe you're struggling with a situation like my friend Gene's. I first met Gene when his wife, a member of the church, asked me to visit him and try to lead him to Christ. Whenever he saw me coming, he would rush out the back door or into a back room.

I finally caught him one evening at dinnertime and had a pleasant visit. I just tried to make friends with him and didn't talk much about the church. After I left, he told his wife, "I think I'll go to church with you just to see what that fellow has to say. He didn't even talk to me about church."

A few visits later, Gene declared his faith in Christ and was baptized. As he continued to come to church, he faced another problem. God was stirring his nest. One night whenever he tried to sleep, his eyes popped open because God was reminding him of something that he had not surrendered to Him. Gene later told me, "I got up, went out into the backyard, and paced back and forth talking to God. Finally, I surrendered the thing God had pinpointed and went back to bed. My eyes popped open again. God reminded me of another area of my life that I still controlled instead of letting Him. So I got up again and paced the backyard until I surrendered that part of my life. That went on all night. I never got any sleep because as soon as I settled one thing, God would bring up something else."

He went on, "After another sleepless night and several more trips to the backyard, I felt like I was playing checkers with God. Just when I thought I had made a good move, God would jump over three of my checkers all the way to kings' row. Finally, it came down to the last issue that I was not willing to deal with—tithing. I told God, 'I've lived forty-two years without tithing, and I'm not about to start now!'

"God replied, 'Grave clothes don't have any pockets.'

"'Okay, God, I get the point. I'll start tithing, too.'"

Only after yielding this final aspect did Gene receive any rest.

Take a moment to reflect on where you are in your life journey. You may not be a baby eagle, but are you going through the same experience of having your Father stir your nest? Do you feel that you are "losing your checkers" to God? Maybe you are currently trying to consolidate your assets rather than surrender them to the Lord. Is He asking you to surrender something you hold dear so you can be fully dedicated to Him and His cause? It doesn't matter what your issue is—you must surrender it to

God if it is keeping you from being obedient to Him and allowing Him to work abundantly in your life. You may have reservations about walking away from lifelong investments, but God is challenging you to a new possibility.

Look up! There is much more that God has in mind for you.

LET'S GET PERSONAL HERE

1. What uncomfortable changes have you experienced that made you question God? Did you think at the time that God was involved in those changes?
2. When was the last time God stirred your nest? Make a list of the times in your life you can now see were nest stirrings.
3. What lies in your heart that you don't want God to expose? A secret sin? Unresolved conflict with a person? Your doubt? Your fears? A selfish dream?
4. Why do you think God is stirring your nest now? God stirs your nest to get your undivided attention. Whether it is an unresolved issue or simply the way to fulfill God's plan for your life, consider the reasons. Is God stirring your nest to help you follow Him? Do you need to grow in Christ, launch out on a new adventure, or make a significant life change?
5. What is your attitude going to be in response to God?

CHAPTER 2

IS THAT YOU, GOD?

Whenever you face trials . . . your faith develops perseverance.
— JAMES 1:2-3

What could God have to do with disquieting or troubling circumstances in your life? Everything! What could God have to do with the stirrings in your heart? They call you to His eternal purpose. God is intent on your knowing Him and joining Him in His plan.

Do you remember when you were a child and your brother or sister hurt you? Your strongest accusation was that he or she harmed you "on purpose." If the action had been an accident, it would have been excusable, but if intent was involved, blame was going to fly.

In the same way, we struggle to understand how God — as our loving Father — could be involved in anything that we don't think is good in our lives. We surmise that God never *causes* anything negative, but maybe He *allows* it. We presume that He would never wound us on purpose — but at times, God initiates pain in our lives for a better purpose. God is always a purposeful God, even when we can't fully comprehend His reasons.

Does God always have our best interests at heart? Of course. Do we always recognize His actions as the best option for our lives? Not always. God tells us that His way of thinking is on a different plane than ours, so it's always possible that we will misinterpret God's perfect will as an undesirable situation (see Isaiah 55:8-9).

Let's look at a biblical example. God frequently stirred the nest of Joseph, one of Israel's sons, to make him a leader and save his own family. Joseph's brothers betrayed him by throwing him into a pit and later selling him to merchants (see Genesis 37:24,28). The merchants took him to Egypt, where God prospered Joseph. Then Joseph was falsely accused of rape by Potiphar's wife and thrown into a dungeon for more than two years. God blessed Joseph for trusting Him, but in the process Joseph suffered at the rock bottom of a pit and as a slave in a dungeon. Eventually, Joseph recognized that God meant for him to suffer in order to spare nations from a famine. He told his brothers, "You intended to harm me, but God intended it for good to accomplish what is now being done, the saving of many lives" (Genesis 50:20).

I was resting in a beautiful valley in a communist country. Surrounding hills obstructed my view as if I were in the center of a massive nest. And I felt secure being in the middle of where God wanted me that day. In a summer absent of college classes or job obligations, my two friends and I blazed a trail where no Christian had set foot in the past century. In the past few days, we had told several people in the countryside about Jesus. "Jesus — is He one of your American friends?" was a common response from these people who had never heard His name. A few joyfully received God's salvation.

As I was resting, a police jeep swiftly approached us. The officers interrogated us separately, asking who we were and what we were doing. They knew that we had given Christian literature to those we met, and I began to shake. I juggled prayer and decision making with appropriately answering the barrage of questions from the policemen. They confiscated part of our resources and threatened to arrest us if we did not leave the area. We felt like we were obedient to God in being there but needed to respect the authorities by moving on. It was painful, but these were the first steps of God working even greater things through us. We became less ashamed to suffer and more bold to witness. As a result, we led scores of people to salvation, started churches, and I wrote down 328 extraordinary things that God performed through us that summer.

Have you ever felt like God brought you to rock bottom in your life — to a place where the only means of escape was looking up? Trials and pain are not God's punishment to push you away from Him. On the contrary, He causes you to become dissatisfied with your situation in order to push you toward Him and bring you into His peace, the kind that comes only with your obedience.

> My son, do not make light of the Lord's discipline,
>> and do not lose heart when he rebukes you,
> because the Lord disciplines those he loves,
>> and he punishes everyone he accepts as a son.

> Endure hardship as discipline; God is treating you as sons.
> (Hebrews 12:5-7)

Jesus reminded the apostle Paul, "It is hard for you to kick against the goads" (Acts 26:14). A goad is a sharp metal point that farmers placed on the end of a long pole to prod stubborn animals, such as oxen, to keep moving.[1] It's easier to recognize God's blessings as evidence of His love, but His discipline is an equally valid verification of His love.

In these times of anxiety, we need to decide what we want from God: to be comforted or to be conformed to His will. God may give you both, but which one is your goal? If you choose comfort, you may not be ready to be conformed to His likeness. Choosing comfort over conformity to God's will may be tempting, but comfort tends to thwart our spiritual progress. Discomfort, however, builds the desire within us to soar to higher altitudes. God can deliver us from any trial when He deems fit, so until He does so, we should choose to conform to His plan through the refining pain of the moment (see 2 Peter 2:9).

God conforms us to His character through uncomfortable trials, as described in Proverbs 17:3: "The crucible for silver and the furnace for gold, but the LORD tests the heart." The metal must be heated hot enough to cleanse it of impurities or to bend it into a desired shape. To use another analogy, as clay in the Potter's hands, shouldn't we let Him break, mold, and reshape our lives instead of asking Him to return us to our comfortable state as an unused, nonconformed lump (see Jeremiah 18:4-6)? God is making us Christlike in the process.

As a nation, Israel could not have conformed to God's plan for them if they had remained comfortably in Egypt. They had to leave Egypt to go to the Promised Land. Likewise, we cannot grow up to fly as eagles if we insist on staying in the secure nest of God's protection.

UNDERSTANDING GOD'S STIRRINGS

God wants you to grow closer to Him, but if you don't respond positively to His offer, He may continue to stir your nest so that you will pay attention. Some of His stirrings are external, while others are more internal.

Do you relate to any of the following external stirrings?

- Troubled personal relationships in your life
- Family members' decisions that affect you
- A sudden financial change
- Health problems
- Setbacks at work

Maybe you are experiencing more internal stirrings:

- Deep unfulfilled longings
- A vision of better things
- The exciting prospect of living up to your God-given potential
- Dreams you thought had already died that still come back to mind

As the male eagle flies past its offspring with enticing cuisine just out of reach, so God may be stirring you with external or internal desires that will move you toward His plan for your life, for your good and His glory. God wants you to connect your present situation with His stirrings so you can get in step with His purpose for your life. His stirrings are always a result of His love. God is not teasing you. He is offering you a chance to grow.

Do you envy any Christian mentors, maybe overlooking the stirrings they endured to mature? In Genesis 4, Cain had a younger brother Abel, who seemed able to do everything right. Cain was a farmer and gave some of his produce to God as an offering. Abel was a shepherd and did one better: He offered the best sheep he had to God. God was more pleased with Abel's offering, so Cain became enraged. Listening to God's gentle questions and dialoguing with Abel did not relieve Cain of his jealousy, so Cain murdered Abel. God harshly disciplined Cain by making him a nomad with difficult work to do.

Cain's most obvious offense was murder, but the underlying problem was that he envied his brother's walk with God. It's good to learn from godly men and women and even follow their example, but be who God wants *you* to be. God doesn't want you to be just like them. I'm similar to Avery and have learned a lot from him, but I'm not supposed to imitate everything he does. The Lord doesn't stir you to become like the apostle Paul or Billy Graham; He stirs you to become like Him.

Is God Stirring Your Nest?

Has God ever stirred your nest? For many people, their own salvation was the first time they experienced God's initiative in their lives. But as you grow in your relationship with God, you can become attuned to God's stirrings.

As I prepared for a plane trip, God impressed me to witness to whomever sat beside me. Turns out I was sitting next to a light heavyweight boxer and his trainer. I tried to be friendly and looked for a chance to tell them about Christ, but nothing I said seemed to open the door to talk naturally about spiritual things. Finally the boxer asked me what I did. I replied, "I wrote a book called *MasterLife* and lead a seminar based on it.² It teaches you how to master life." In unison they turned and asked, "How?" Then I told them about Christ.

The boxer said, "You know, that happened to my father not long ago, and he has really changed."

I responded, "It sounds like God is working around you and in your life." (However, I would never have guessed that from our conversation thus far.)

"Yes," he replied. "You know, a friend of mine was driving down I-85 and just pulled over to the side of the road and prayed. He is not the same man. He won't go to bars or run around with me anymore."

"God is really working around your life, isn't He?" I said. "Do you know what I prayed before getting on this flight? I prayed that God would let me sit beside someone with whom He is working."

"Wow!" he exclaimed. "That's heavy!" Then he added, "I saw your Bible beneath your seat."

I shared with them that we are all sinners but that Christ died for our sins—He is willing to forgive us—and He rose from the dead to save us. I said, "God makes us His children when we respond to His offer. We need to do three things. First, we must ask God to forgive us our sins since Jesus died for them. Second, we must turn from our sins and follow Him. Third, we must receive the living Christ into our hearts as our Savior and Lord so we can live for Him." I showed them how to pray a simple prayer, and by the time the plane landed both men had prayed to receive Christ.

The process of becoming Christ's disciple starts with a new birth. Perhaps God has been working around your life and stirring your nest so you will question whether you have a personal relationship with Him (see 2 Corinthians 13:5). If so, wouldn't this be a good time to bow your head, confess your sin, and ask for God's forgiveness and salvation through Christ? If you have questions, contact a pastor who can show you in the Bible what you need to do.

IS THAT YOU, GOD?

If God has already brought you to salvation, be aware that He is not finished with you yet. God still wants to get your attention because He wants to involve you in His purposes. What do you do when you realize that God is stirring your nest? You can't just dismiss it as an inconvenient happenstance or as simple cause and effect. But how can you know whether God is bringing about the changes in your life? Could it be the result of your own mistakes or, worse yet, Satan's activity? If you are not sure, think about the last thing God told you to do that you haven't yet done. Usually that is where we get off track—the place where we last disobeyed.

A student leader in Kansas City, Missouri, Jamie Clark kept wondering why God was not revealing more of what He wanted her to do with her life. Each time she asked, instead of getting the broad answers she expected, God reminded her of several notes of encouragement He had previously asked her to write. Jamie would think, *Yeah, yeah, I'll do that*, but as one thing or another came up, the notes were pushed aside and forgotten.

Yet every time she inquired about God's plan for her life, she heard Him saying, *Those notes, remember those notes.* She realized that God was saying, *You may think it's a little thing, but it's a big thing to me.*

She thought, *If I don't do the things that I think are little things, then how can I do the other things God needs me to do?* God brought Matthew 25:21 to mind: "You have been faithful with a few things; I will put you in charge of many things." When she obeyed with the smaller things, God showed her His bigger plan for her life.

Read slowly through the following criteria and ask God to confirm if He is the one stirring your nest.

How to Know God Is Stirring Your Nest

- When you experience an inward restlessness that will not go away no matter what you do. As you pray, you realize that God is persistently asking you to do something that you didn't initiate.
- When the Holy Spirit confirms that your stirring is from God through portions of Scripture (that you didn't manipulate to say what you wanted to hear).
- When circumstances collaborate with what God has been saying to you through Scripture, prayer, and godly people. Be careful, however, not to take circumstances or godly counsel alone, since people may try to reflect what they think you want them to say instead of what God wants.
- When you sense God is challenging you to do things that you think are impossible, causing you to face a crisis of faith when you decide whether or not you will believe God.
- When you progressively pursue God's will about the stirring, and the sense of rightness and peace becomes stronger.

- When this new stirring lines up with the spiritual markers in your life—times when you knew that you heard from God and did His will.
- When the stirring leads you toward fulfilling God's ultimate purpose instead of selfish goals.

ALL STIRRINGS ARE NOT FROM GOD

You may currently be experiencing many troubles, but this does not always indicate God's activity. How can you be sure that what you are experiencing is not a consequence of your own mistakes or the world or the Devil? Consider the following guidelines that may indicate that God is not the source of your discomfort. Bring your stirrings into the presence of God and ask Him to interpret them for you.

How to Know God Is Not Stirring Your Nest

- When the voice is insistent, strident, and urgent that you do something immediately and tells you that you don't have time to fully explore whether it is from God.
- When the Scriptures warn against the actions you are contemplating.
- When circumstances and the advice from others do not resonate with what God is saying in the Word and by His Spirit.
- When you feel confident that you can do what you are being asked to do in your own strength.
- When you spiritually resist what the insistent voice is saying, and it goes away.
- When what you are being stirred to do has no correlation with your spiritual markers—the times you knew God was speaking to you and you did His will.
- When the opportunity does not accomplish the long-range purposes of God, or it will bring someone else more glory than God.

If God Is Stirring Your Nest

What do you think? Is God stirring your nest? After reading the signals, maybe you've come to the conclusion that God isn't stirring your nest; you're just at a decision point in life. If you feel God is not directly initiating a change, recognize that He is still interested in your situation. The Bible tells us in Philippians 4:6-7 to be anxious about nothing, but rather to present your thoughts and struggles to God. But get ready because God will stir your nest at some time in the future. It's His way.

If you do sense that God is stirring your nest now, what should you do next? Here are several things you can do:

1. Acknowledge to God that you recognize He is initiating a change.
2. Thank God that He cares enough to get involved in your life.
3. Surrender your changes, your future, and your life to Him.
4. Ask God to show you why He is stirring your nest.
5. Ask God to reveal to you what He wants you to do next.
6. Wait on the Lord to reveal Himself, His purposes, and His ways.
7. Do immediately and absolutely whatever He asks. When God stirs your nest, He is expecting you to change.

Discerning the Stirring

At different seasons in life, God stirs you to do different things. He may want to change your character, your vocation, your location, your direction, or your life's calling.

Each time that God has stirred my life, I have discovered that He is getting me ready for my next assignment. I have learned through hard experiences that it is much easier to obey Him and follow Him than to resist His activity in my life. One time God stirred me to leave a situation, like when He called Moses to go back to Egypt. In a different situation, God stirred my nest by commanding me to stay in the middle of the problems and deal with the difficulties, as Moses did when the Israelites criticized him.

In our second four-year term as missionaries, Shirley and I moved with our five children to East Java, Indonesia, to start churches. We were the only missionaries among several million people, and we felt called to share God's love with them. Less than a year into the term, however, Shirley dropped a bombshell on me. "I am overwhelmed," she said. "I can't take this anymore." I suggested several things that I could change, but by the time she admitted the depth of her struggle, it was too late for simple answers. I had the depressing thought that we might have to quit being missionaries and return to America.

As we talked, I realized I had been part of the problem. I had been so busy that I had failed to help her deal with the problems she faced. She was homeschooling three of our children for the first time, in addition to taking care of our two other children still in diapers. The entire eight months we lived in our house, she had to endure workmen who were underfoot making renovations. Often away from home, I had been so preoccupied with starting churches and leading a national research project that I was oblivious to the warning signs.

As we prayed, I began to ask God what we could do. Several times I had turned down offers to teach in the Indonesian seminary because I wanted to start churches on the front lines where no missionaries had gone. Yet God used our family's situation to lead me to become a seminary professor in a city where Shirley could share the teaching load with other mothers. At the time, I did not identify that situation as the stirring of God because it was not what I wanted to do. However, as we followed His leadership as best we could under the circumstances, I discovered that it *was* His plan. When I was elected president of the seminary a few years later, I realized that the experience of teaching for two years was much-needed preparation for me to lead the seminary in a different direction.

The next stirring, when God called me to endure difficulties, occurred a few years later, after we had radically changed the seminary to focus on theological education by extension. This was necessary in order to train the leaders of the village churches that had tripled in number during the previous five years. I faced extreme pressure from some of the Indonesian leadership to reverse the changes we had made, yet we were convinced that God had led us to make the changes in the first place and that we were still in His will. I was, however, feeling overwhelmed, as Shirley had been earlier. One day after a particularly grueling session with the leadership, I told God, "I've had it. If one more thing happens, I am out of here." As usual, one more thing happened.

I sought the Lord's guidance in the Bible. I expected Him to comfort me or tell me to leave the seminary, but He desired to change me instead of the situation. I read the following words in my regular Bible reading:

> If you have raced with men on foot
>   and they have worn you out,
>   how can you compete with horses?
> If you stumble in safe country,
>   how will you manage in the thickets by the Jordan?
>   (Jeremiah 12:5)

I complained, "Oh, Lord, You don't mean it is going to get worse."

Yes, He replied, *it is going to get worse. Can't you see that I am preparing you for much more difficult tasks that I have for you in the future? Buck up; it is time for you to persevere through these hard times and finish the job I sent you here to do.*

In this second case, the troubles were not the stirring of God to get me ready to go somewhere else. On the contrary, God was using the stirrings to shape my character for future assignments—and He told me so emphatically. Years later, as vice president of overseas operations for the International Mission Board, I faced many more difficult times as we made radical changes in our worldwide missionary strategy. I realized why God had kept me in the difficult situation at the seminary years before. He was developing my character to match a later assignment.

When I graduated from high school, I had already recognized God's call on my life to serve in vocational ministry, but I knew nothing of what God held in my future except for the university I was about to attend. I thought I would probably become a pastor. When the opportunity came that summer for me to preach my first sermon at a church, I bombed it. I told God if that experience was any indication of my future, I was in big trouble.

The next day I toured a museum that recounted Christian history and read missionary David Livingstone's remark etched on the wall: "People talk of the sacrifice I have made in spending so much of my life in Africa. . . . It is emphatically no sacrifice. Say rather it is a privilege."[3] After surveying items from Rachel Scott, who was shot at Columbine High School for professing her belief in God, I ventured out to the museum's prayer garden, questioning what role God wanted me to serve in life. In the garden were several missions displays identifying other nations of the world, their religions, and the number of people who had yet to know Christ there. As I talked to God, I had a growing sense that I would spend part of my life in another country doing missions work. Ultimately, I came to a simple prayer of surrender. I stopped telling God what I wanted to do with my life, and I started listening to His direction. I prayed, "God, whatever You want to do with my life, I'm willing."

That meeting with God influenced my future decisions to share Jesus with people in eastern Asia for the next two summers; marry Allison, who was one of my college teammates on the missions trip; and serve as a minister in a local Chinese church while I completed college. I don't know all that the future holds, but I learned that when God stirs your nest, you'd better listen to Him.

STIRRED FOR LIFE

Perhaps you say, "I have grown. I am following God's will, yet I'm going through all these troubling times. Why?" God's stirrings certainly aren't always brought on by our disobedience or error; He may be stirring you because you have been faithful with little, and He wants to make you responsible for more. God is likely doing something new in your life to make you more complete.

You may be going through a time like my friend Dick, and it wasn't because he had done anything wrong. He worked for the U.S. Justice Department at the time the Soviet Union began to fall apart. He was asked to help two of the satellite countries develop new legal institutions from the ground up, including advising on the content of constitutions. He realized that this could be the reason he was born — to help new countries guarantee the rights of their citizens, including religious liberty.

Despite this uniquely important work, he felt God stirring his well-worn nest of nearly thirty years of government service to use his legal expertise for more intentional kingdom purposes. Over time he discerned God specifically leading him to use his past experience to help organizations and countries with legal advice as a Christian lawyer. He moved with his wife to central Asia and started discipling young lawyers, equipping them to help construct the foundations for societies based on the rule of law and principles of integrity. God is still using him in remarkable ways — more than he had ever imagined — making an impact not just in the former Soviet Union but also around the world.

God stirred Dick's nest not as a punishment but to make him more productive for His kingdom. He ultimately realized that everything he had ever done within the legal profession, including service as a judge and prosecutor, was in preparation for God's special purpose for his life of ministry to others. Jesus said that God prunes the branches of His people so that they will become more fruitful (see John 15:2).

Whenever God stirs your nest, get ready for change.

LET'S GET PERSONAL HERE

1. Who is stirring your nest — God, Satan, or a particular person(s)? Why do you say that?
2. Regardless of how you answered question 1, do you more strongly desire comfort from God or conformity to God's will? How do you prove that by your actions?
3. How is God stirring your nest? What do you do when you realize that God is stirring your nest?
4. What changes is God asking you to make?
5. What do you need to adjust in order to obey God's stirring?

PART TWO

GOD HOVERS OVER YOU

Like an eagle that stirs up its nest,
That hovers over its young,
He spread His wings and caught them,
He carried them on His pinions.
The LORD alone guided him,
And there was no foreign god with him.

— DEUTERONOMY 32:11-12, NASB

HOW BIG IS YOUR GOD?

Who has measured the waters in the hollow of his hand, or with the breadth of his hand marked off the heavens? Who has held the dust of the earth in a basket, or weighed the mountains on the scales and the hills in a balance?

— ISAIAH 40:12

After the parent eagle has made life miserable for the eaglets by stirring the nest, she begins her second strategy to help them live up to their potential. She hovers above them. Perhaps for the first time the eaglets realize how huge their mother is. Her wings can measure up to eight feet from tip to tip[1]—approximately the width of a school bus. As she flutters her wings, she demonstrates authority and power to her young, as if to say, *Never fear; Mother's here.*

Do you remember as a child feeling peace and relief when your mother assured you of her presence and attention? Perhaps she even kissed away the hurt. The situation had not improved, but you felt better. That is what happens to the eaglets. The parents' hovering above them does not relieve any of the eaglets' pain, but it shows them how to soar out of the nest. By circling high above them, the parents demonstrate their goal for the eaglets before teaching them how to fly. The eaglets' circumstances still are uncomfortable, but they see that the ones who have stirred their nest also have a plan to better their future.

Like an eaglet, you may have been content and safe in your nest before God stirred it. Are you asking, "God, why don't You do something?" He is! He is hovering above you to calm you down and to invite you further into His will. External change is inevitable, but internal change is a choice. Make the choice to trust God in your adversity. Don't seek quick fixes from God; seek Him!

God never forsakes us when He stirs our nests, so the last thing we should do is forsake Him in our adversity. His stirring is the first step to move us through His plan for our lives, which He follows up with His next step—hovering over us. Look up at Him hovering above you and recognize that He can handle your adversity, that He is present, and that He is worthy to be followed. You could be at the waiting stage before adolescence in the middle of the diagram on page 20.

God's hovering may seem like a pause in the process of what He is doing by stirring your nest—a painful, confusing pause. God seems to like the pause button more than the fast-forward button. So it's tempting to pray, "Okay, God, You have my attention by stirring me. Now will You fix the problem?" God's purpose in stirring is to improve your relationship with Him more than to solve your immediate problem. God hovers over you not necessarily to change your activities, like a job or location, because if He instantly healed the stirring, you would likely seek Him less intently. Sometimes He hovers over you just to capture your attention more intently and help you grow in worship.

He did that with my wife, Allison, when she was in college. Warts covered the bottom of her left foot, causing extreme pain and nearly immobilizing her. For the entire summer, she was unable to walk without intense pain, which killed her plans for a job, cross-country running, and some travel. Rather, she sat at home studying the Bible and reading a plethora of Christian classics. Though it was a slow, painful process, Allison reflects on that summer when God hovered over her as a period when she grew most deeply in her walk with Him.

God Hovered over the Israelites

While they were still in slavery's nest, the Israelites looked up at their heavenly Creator's great hovering power in each of the ten plagues He brought on the Egyptians, their oppressors. The first two plagues—turning water to blood and an invasion of frogs—were duplicated by Pharaoh's sorcerers, but still Pharaoh pleaded with Moses to remove them. When the sorcerers could not duplicate the third plague—swarms of gnats—they told Pharaoh, "This is the finger of God" (Exodus 8:19). In the fourth plague—flies—God made a distinction between the Israelites and Egyptians, and the flies did not appear in Goshen, where the Israelites lived. In every miraculous plague from then on, God hovered over and protected the Israelites while punishing the Egyptians. God killed the livestock of Egypt, but none of Israel's livestock died. God sent boils on the Egyptians and then sent the worst hailstorm that had ever fallen on Egypt—while the sun shone on God's chosen people.

At this point God told Moses to remind the Israelites that He had hardened Pharaoh's heart so that they could tell their children and grandchildren about His miracles and know that He was God (see Exodus 10:1-2). The last three plagues were the most extreme. God sent the worst locust plague Egypt had ever experienced. Then He sent three days of total darkness over Egypt (although Israel had light). With each plague Pharaoh seemed to concede, but once the plague was over, he changed his mind. The final plague was the death of all the firstborn of the Egyptians and their livestock; the people of Israel were spared because they obeyed God and sacrificed a Passover lamb.

Throughout this process, Moses and his people often despaired and complained over their plight, and Pharaoh continually changed his mind. God told them that it was "so that my wonders may be multiplied in Egypt" (Exodus 11:9). How long do you have to sit in a stirred-up nest? Only God knows. God required the Israelites to wait beneath His presence of cloud by day and fire by night in the wilderness for hours, days, and sometimes even weeks (see Numbers 9:21-22).

Before Jesus ascended to heaven, He told His disciples to witness about Him in Jerusalem, Judea, Samaria, and the ends of the earth (see Acts 1:8).

He clearly commanded them, however, to wait in Jerusalem for the Holy Spirit's filling before they obeyed His commission (see Acts 1:4). God calls us to wait patiently in His presence—yet this does not mean that we are to be passive. Patience in the Bible is active. Patience means bearing up under a heavy burden. It means endurance and persistence. Many times God instructs His people to exercise faith by waiting on Him.

God used the metaphor of the eagle in Isaiah 40:30-31 to show the importance of waiting in the presence of the Lord:

> Though youths grow weary and tired,
> And vigorous young men stumble badly,
> Yet those who wait for the LORD
> Will gain new strength;
> They will mount up with wings like eagles,
> They will run and not get tired,
> They will walk and not become weary. (NASB)

You may be tempted to give up during this waiting period. You may feel that God should *do something*—but He will fulfill His purposes; just wait on Him. In the movie *The Karate Kid*, Daniel wants to compete; he grows impatient because his instructor makes him wax a car, not realizing that by doing so he is perfecting moves for karate. When young people try to solve their problems their own way, they grow tired and weary. The secret is waiting on the Lord to act. If you wait, "the Creator of the ends of the earth [who] does not become weary or tired" will give you new strength (Isaiah 40:28, NASB). Pastor Andy Stanley said, "Waiting time is not wasted time for anyone in whose heart God has placed a vision. Difficult time. Painful time. Frustrating time. But not wasted time."[2]

In the next phase of the eagle's development (part 3) you will see how God takes you on His wings. For now, you are to wait in God's presence while He fulfills His promise: "He gives strength to the weary, and to him who lacks might He increases power" (Isaiah 40:29, NASB). Look for what is coming—you will fly like eagles, run like young men, and walk without growing weary.

God Hovers over Us

Psalm 91:4 says that God hovers over us: "He will cover you with his feathers, and under his wings you will find refuge." Look at the Lord stretching His wings beside and above you and be amazed at what it is like to follow such a magnificent God. Jesus perfectly lived our Father's will on earth, "leaving you an example, that you should follow in his steps" (1 Peter 2:21). God stretches His wings in flight first to model for you how to fly.

God Broods over Us

In a process known as brooding, the mother eagle surrounds her eaglets for several weeks, providing all that is necessary for their growth during their first crucial stage of life. It is not until the eaglets are ready to fly that their mother stops brooding and begins hovering above them.[3] If the eaglet wants to stay close to its parents, it needs to learn to fly. God's hovering over you is a signal that He's ready for you to move on to the next level of following Him.

A Personal yet Enormous God

Most people would prefer to see an eagle five feet away rather than squint to see the eagle as a speck in the sky—but both views are awe inspiring. As the eagle reveals its grandeur both near and far, God demonstrates His power to us from a distance as well as up close.

Do you view your Creator from a distance without also seeing Him beside you? Or do you view God as your nearby companion without also worshipping Him as the Lord who soars over His universe? "'Am I only a God nearby,' declares the Lord, 'and not a God far away? . . . Do not I fill heaven and earth?'" (Jeremiah 23:23-24). It is important that we stand in awe of God not only for how personally He cares for us but also for how powerfully He rules the vast universe. Sometimes we fear situations and problems in life because we unconsciously regard them as bigger than our God. As Ruthie said to Jeffy in a *Family Circus* cartoon, "It's okay to pray for something little. Everything's little to God."[4] Step back, see the fluttering of God's wings over you, and realize how big your God is!

When my deepest questions go unanswered, I rejoice that I worship One who is bigger than my three-pound brain. If I had God totally figured out, it would mean I worship a tiny God. I do, however, think it's natural and even good to seek answers from God. Job questioned God about why He remained silent during his pain (see Job 30:20). God's answer to Job was, *Do you know who you're talking to? I'm infinitely bigger than you realize.*

One of the hardest questions I ever asked God was, "Why did my father-in-law die?" In our first year of marriage, Allison's dad, Ken, unexpectedly and instantly passed away. I mentally understood the horror, but my heart has never accepted that disaster. I've learned, however, not to seek the *answers* as much as I seek *God*, who can answer all of my questions. The possibility of questions being answered provides a false sense of comfort, while only God can provide peace, even in our ignorance. Though it is fine for me to want to know why God does the things He does, I know I should revere Him and follow Him even if He never answers all my questions.

OUT OF THIS WORLD

Imagine with me just one aspect of God's fluttering His wings — His enormous magnificence. I wish I could describe the greatness of God, but I can't begin to understand it myself. Let's look at just one demonstration of God's greatness: His creation of the universe.

Suppose you wanted to go to the edge of outer space and could travel at the fastest speed ever recorded for a manned vehicle, about forty-seven miles per second.[5] Going that fast, the space shuttle usually takes two days to reach the moon from Earth[6] — but you're going too slow if you want to reach the outer limits of space. Why? You wouldn't live long enough to arrive there. So suppose you could obtain a spacecraft that went the speed of light — 186,200 miles per second.[7] At the speed of light, you would pass the moon in only two seconds, and in 8.3 minutes you would pass the sun. You are reminded of the enormity of space when you pass the sun and realize that more than a million Earths could fit inside it.[8]

When my son Randy was seven years old, he asked how fast light was. I told him, "The speed of light is so fast that if it could go in a circle along the equator, it would travel around the world more than seven times in one second." He paused and then countered, "Wow! If that was a bullet, you'd get shot seven times before you could fall down." Now that *is* fast. Traveling at the speed of light, you could exit our solar system in about four hours and in nearly four years get to the Earth's nearest star beyond the sun, Proxima Centauri.[9] If you reduced our sun to the size of the period at the end of this sentence, Proxima Centauri would be eight miles away,[10] which would take more than seventy-three thousand years to reach traveling in the fastest space vehicle ever made.[11] You could never live long enough to reach the limits of outer space even if you flew at the speed of light! In fact, it would take you more than fourteen thousand years just to escape our Milky Way galaxy—and the Earth is already on the edge of it.[12]

To get an idea of how far the nearest galaxy to ours is, imagine that the distance from the sun to Proxima Centauri, the closest star—which is more than twenty-four trillion miles away—is as far as this book is from your eyes as you read these words. If that were so, the Andromeda galaxy, the nearest major galaxy similar to the Milky Way, would be 150 miles away.[13] Suppose you could call someone in the Andromeda galaxy at the speed of light. It would still take 2.5 million years at the speed of light for someone to hear you say hello.[14] It would take another 2.5 million years for you to hear his or her response. That is five million years just to say hello. Talk about an expensive phone call!

This galaxy and everything you can see in space with the naked eye are part of the Local Group,[15] which includes the thirty galaxies nearest the Milky Way. Although we can't comprehend that space could be so vast, this observable group really is no more than the front porch of space. The Local Group, in fact, is less than one-tenth of 1 percent of the distance of the observable universe,[16] which is estimated to be thirteen billion light-years in diameter,[17] containing about 70,000,000,000,000,000,000,000 stars within ten billion galaxies.[18] That huge number of stars—each one distant from the next—is equal to the approximate number of tiny grains of sand on the earth.[19]

So how does God look at the vastness and complexity of this universe He created? Isaiah 40:12 says the One who spoke the universe into existence measures it by the "breadth of his hand." God looks down through all of space at a commonplace galaxy with an ordinary solar system that revolves around a third-rate star and includes a planet that we call Earth. God so loved the people of that earth that He gave His only Son to save them (see John 3:16). I can't fathom such greatness and such love, yet God's magnitude is only one aspect of His many inestimable traits!

One of the practical ways I see God hovering over me is how He has blessed my family through the past century. I don't know how many generations ago it was when the first person in my family accepted Christ, but I am thankful to my forebearers. As a result, all these years later, my parents, siblings, and I have decided to become followers of Christ, as have most of my relatives. In Exodus 20:6, God promised that He would love the next thousand generations of those who love Him. So if you do not have a Christian heritage, take heart that through God's grace you can leave a godly inheritance to your family and descendants. Perhaps you will find strength in a prayer that God has given to my granddad through Scripture: "Even when I am old and gray, do not forsake me, O God, till I declare your power to the next generation, your might to all who are to come" (Psalm 71:18).

If God takes care of the gigantic universe, can you trust Him to care for you and your problems? Of course! God's purpose in hovering over you is not just to relieve your anxiety but to demonstrate how you can leave your nest to follow Him as He leads you to His ultimate will through life's changes. So when God flutters His wings, you can trust Him through the changes you're experiencing.

GOD'S PLANS ARE GOOD

Although change is inevitable, God's strength is infinite. Change can confuse us because the only sure thing about change is uncertainty. You may not understand the details of your situation, but you can believe that the power of God will help you in all your circumstances if you trust Him.

Changes occur in everyone's life, but you must recognize that you don't grow by inactive observation. You grow, rather, by faith and confidence in Him. So when God hovers over you, rise up!

Changes can appear to be positive or negative, but when God is involved, the end result is always for good. "'I know the plans I have for you,' declares the LORD, 'plans to prosper you and not to harm you, plans to give you hope and a future'" (Jeremiah 29:11). I heard Bishop Kenneth Ulmer, pastor of Faithful Central Bible Church in Los Angeles, paint a brilliant word picture of these verses that has buoyed me along as I wait and watch for Him to do His work in and through me. Ulmer said that the word for *plans* is a word picture of a tapestry that God is weaving. Your life may look like a mess from the back side of the tapestry, but if you wait, you will see what God sees on the other side — a beautiful life tapestry that He is weaving.[20]

Certainly, the people of Israel saw their situation as a mess when God gave them this promise. They were in exile in Babylon, and this was God's promise to bring them home. Ulmer said the rest of the verse is a word picture of a rowboat moving toward the tapestry — the fulfillment of God's plan. You are rowing a rowboat with your back to the future and looking at your past. But, he said, "the picture here is of a rope pulling you toward God's design. God has a rope of hope on your boat that is pulling you to your destiny!"

God gives you great promises, like Jeremiah 29:11, to help you persevere in following Him through change. He is always doing for you what He knows is best, though your present situation may seem to indicate otherwise. God does want to bless you, but the process to that end is not always quick or pleasant.

When God hovers over His people and leads them to places He has promised, the ultimate purpose is always for them to know Him better, obey Him more carefully, worship Him more sincerely, and glorify Him more constantly.

LET'S GET PERSONAL HERE

1. How long are you willing to sit in a stirred-up nest?
2. What similarities and differences do you see between the ways your parents cared for you and how God cares for you?
3. Which of God's hoverings do you need to focus on more: His intimate relationship with you or the distant grandeur of His nature? Why?
4. Do you view God's hovering over you as an invitation to join His agenda or as an interruption of your own agenda? Explain your feelings.
5. Check your prayers. Are you asking God to change things back to the way they used to be, or do you trust Him with the new things He's doing in your life? How do you think you should be praying as you wait?

CHAPTER 4

GROWING IN GOD'S WAYS

[God] made known his ways to Moses,
his deeds to the people of Israel.
— PSALM 103:7

When I was a boy, I often went fishing with Papaw, my granddad, who was a consummate fisherman. Even when no one else caught fish, he did. I never remember him coming home without fish, and usually he would have a tub full. I was a novice when he began to take me fishing with him. He would help me find a good place, bait my hook, and then leave me to do the rest. I was able to catch a few fish when he guided me each step of the way. But when I went fishing by myself, I did not do so well. Over time I learned that Papaw used different bait and tackle for different kinds of fish. Somehow he knew where to find each kind of fish because he had learned how fish live—where they stayed at certain times of the day, what they ate, and even what artificial lures attracted them. I did okay with the *acts* of fishing when he helped me, but he knew the *ways* of fish, which enabled him to thrive at fishing.

Anyone can see the *acts* of God, but He wants you to know His *ways*. It's one thing to recognize that God is stirring you; it's another thing to understand God's hovering over you and what He's doing in light of His ways. God's ways are related to His character, and you know them only by His self-revelation or by a longtime relationship with Him. For example, if you hear that your father has done something that seems totally out of character, you will say, "No, my dad would never do that!" At the very least you will withhold judgment until you can ask your father if he did it and why. You say that because you know him and have seen his actions under all kinds of circumstances. However, if you try to understand God by interpreting only one or two actions, you may totally miss what He is doing.

A man watched a carpenter build a table. He thought it was the strangest table he had ever seen. So he asked the carpenter, "Why are you building a table like that?" to which the carpenter replied, "This isn't a table; it is going to be a chest of drawers." Then it all made sense.

If you don't understand God's actions right now, consider what you know of His ways and ask what He is building. In Deuteronomy 32:11 God told us the four ways He leads us from the stirring to soaring:

1. God stirs our nest to prepare us for growth and change.
2. He hovers over us during a time of waiting to build patience, wisdom, and perseverance in us. If we do not give up but persistently follow Him, He develops our character and gives us faith to pursue Him even more.
3. He takes us on His wings and teaches us to fly through trial and error.
4. He is the wind that empowers us to soar, even above storms.

When you don't understand what God is doing in your life, go back and look at your situation in light of God's revealed ways. This chapter offers a real-life example to show how God hovers over us to teach us His ways and to equip us to serve Him. In one encounter at the burning bush, God gave Moses an understanding of His ways that was later refined in Deuteronomy 32:11. The longer we walk with God, the more we see how He is teaching us the same lessons over and over.

UNDERSTANDING THE WAYS OF GOD

A few months after God had hovered over millions of people through ten plagues, the Israelites began to understand the person behind the name of the One they worshipped. Even some Egyptians realized God's ways were higher than their gods and integrated with the Israelites (see Exodus 12:37-38).

But God had to prepare Moses—by stirring his nest again and hovering over him—before he could lead Israel through its bigger challenge: crossing the Red Sea. God usually hovers over individuals before showing His power to the masses. God had stirred Moses at age forty to leave Egypt. Moses had understood the agony of patience while he stayed in Midian for forty years after trying to redeem Israel his way—by killing an Egyptian who tortured an Israelite slave. Now at age eighty, Moses was again stirred at the burning bush (see Exodus 3:2), where God commanded him to lead the Israelites out of Egypt—this time according to His ways. Then God hovered over him in Exodus 4:1-17 to encourage him to return to Egypt.

Moses needed his personal hovering experience with God before he was confident enough to lead others. Moses had questioned God: "What if they do not believe me or listen to me and say, 'The LORD did not appear to you'?" (Exodus 4:1). God knew it was time to take Moses to school on His ways, so He showed him five methods by which He deals with us as individuals. You have the privilege of learning these ways of God through Moses' experience, or you can learn them the hard way through your own experience. Either way, they must be learned if you want God to use you to lead others.

Way of God #1: God takes very ordinary things or people and does extraordinary things with them.
God told Moses to throw his ordinary shepherd's staff on the ground. He did, and it turned into a snake. God told him to pick it up by the tail. Moses was reluctant, but when he picked it up, God turned it back into Moses' ordinary staff (see Exodus 4:4). God showed him that He uses ordinary things to do His extraordinary will.

God essentially asked, *Moses, what is in your hand?* (see Exodus 4:2).
Moses answered, "A staff."

Give it to Me, Moses.

"Yes, Lord, here it is."

God took Moses' staff and with it led the Israelites through the Red
Sea and the wilderness.

Throughout the Bible, God asked people, *What is in your hand?* to
show them that He uses the ordinary to do the supernatural. God took the
widow's last bit of flour and oil and asked her to feed Elijah, and when she
obeyed, He multiplied it every day so that she, her son, and Elijah could
eat for about two years (see 1 Kings 17:1–18:1).[1] God took the slingshot
in David's hand and with it killed Goliath (see 1 Samuel 17:1-58). God
took only three hundred men out of thirty-two thousand and defeated an
incalculable number of Midianites, even though Gideon felt too ordinary
to lead such a battle (see Judges 6:15; 7:1-25). God took the lunch in the
hand of a little boy and fed five thousand men plus many women and
children (see John 6:1-14). God took the fishing net in Peter's hand and
made him a fisher of men; in one day he brought three thousand people to
Christ (see Acts 2:1-41).

God does not need you for anything (see Psalm 50:9-12). He wants you to
follow Him, but you benefit from that commitment more than He does.
God isn't asking for your help because He has a low self-esteem. Rather,
He wants you to be involved in His ways because He loves you. When you
fail to recognize that God is as large as He is, you incorrectly believe you're
essential to God and thus Christianize your efforts to help Him. For example,
some praise songs implore us to "lift Him up," as if He were a manmade idol
and not already sitting on the peak of heaven. Many scriptures refer to God's
voice as booming thunder, yet we think that we must be silent in order to
help God's whispers be heard. When we sing about "magnifying" God, let us
remember we are using a spiritual telescope — not a microscope.[2] The ways
that God interacts with us — and the fact that He communicates with us at
all — are due to His rich mercy.

When you give God what's in your hands, He multiplies your potential beyond your wildest dreams. The First Baptist Church of Springdale, Arkansas, started an extension of their church ten miles from my house in a shopping center in Rogers. It grew rapidly, and they began to raise money for a building. The pastor of the sponsoring church, Ronnie Floyd, preached a sermon on "Special Treasures"—also the name of their building campaign—to ask people to give money for the new church's building. Glendora, a widow, heard his challenge at a luncheon for senior adults and wanted to give. She had so little money, however, that the ladies in her Sunday school class were actually collecting household items to help her set up her home for a planned move back to Illinois.

While Glendora was waiting for her next Social Security check so she would have enough bus fare to return to Illinois, she heard the pastor's challenge about giving sacrificially to "Special Treasures." She felt led to give her wedding ring as her offering. Pastor Floyd was touched with this "widow's mite" and challenged another group of adults in his congregation to redeem the ring. One man could not sleep that night and came to the church office the next morning with $5,000 for the ring, and then he returned it to "Special Treasures."

Before Glendora left, another couple had "purchased" the ring for $10,000 and returned it. She was overcome that her gift had multiplied so much. After she left, another widow gave $20,000 for the ring and returned it. A few days later someone gave $40,000; another person gave $80,000; and someone else "bought" the ring for $160,000—bringing the total given to a phenomenal $315,000! The following week, the ring was purchased for $1,043,000! God multiplies whatever you give to fulfill His purposes.

God is asking you today, *What is in your hand?* No matter how ordinary it may be, God is saying, *Give it to Me,* so He can do out-of-the-ordinary things through you. God's extraordinary power is best displayed through ordinary people in order for Him to get the glory. Do you feel very ordinary? You are exactly at the place where God can use you!

William Booth, founder of the Salvation Army, understood that surrendering to God and walking by faith were the secrets necessary to soar like an eagle. An aged General Booth said,

God has had all there was of me. There have been men with greater brains than I, men with greater opportunities; but from the day I got the poor of London on my heart, and a vision of what Jesus Christ could do with the poor of London, I made up my mind that God would have all of William Booth there was.[3]

The first gift God wants from you is your surrender. Your job is to sign an ordinary blank check of faith and let God fill in the amount. It is His job to cash the check and use you however He desires.

Way of God #2: God wants you to obey His instructions whether or not they make sense to you.
God told Moses, "Put your hand inside your cloak" (Exodus 4:6). When Moses pulled his hand out, he had leprosy. Puzzled, Moses' eyebrows likely shot up. That certainly was not what he was expecting, but God expects us to obey Him even when we don't understand. Too often we say to God, "Tell me what You want me to accomplish, and I'll do it"—by which we usually mean, "Then I'll consider it." Obedience usually requires some knowledge, but complete comprehension is not a prerequisite to obedience. Our obeying God's commands is how He builds our faith in Him. If we knew the outcome before we obeyed God, it wouldn't be faith. God uses our obedience to move us into what He is doing.

Move to a foreign country. Give up your job here, sell your house, and say goodbye forever to your relatives. Get on the highway, and as you're driving, I'll tell you where to build your new home and what you'll do there. If God said that to you today, would you do it? He commanded Abraham to leave everything he knew, but I would probably want it the other way around: "God, I'll do whatever You want; just tell me what it is before I do it." We often flip-flop God's ways: "God, I don't want to go to college until You give me 100 percent confidence which school I should attend and enough scholarships." "God, I know You want me to serve You in a new way, but I can't afford to quit my job without the security of a new one." "God, I'll go wherever You want, but I'm not selling my house until I know where I am going. I don't want to be homeless." If you follow God without knowing where you're going, most people will think you are pitiful. Conversely, God will credit you as righteous, as He did Abraham (see Romans 4:3).

C. T. Studd was a famous cricketer in England whose fame would rival any of our sports heroes today. He grew up in a wealthy family and seemed to have the world on a string when at the age of twenty-five, he gave up cricket to become a missionary to China. While serving in China, he inherited his father's fortune, which was more than enough to pay for his every need on the mission field; he would never have to work or raise support again. As he prayed about it, he sensed that God had given him the opportunity to do what the rich young ruler had failed to do (see Mark 10:17-25). Studd obeyed and gave away his fortune.

In the eyes of the world Studd was a fool. He gave £5,000 to D. L. Moody, an evangelist who had been instrumental in his father's conversion. Moody used the money to begin a training center, which became the Moody Bible Institute. This institute is still training workers more than one hundred years after Moody's death. Studd sent another £5,000 to George Mueller, who used it to house and feed thousands of orphans. Studd gave £8,400 to the Salvation Army, which was used for the poor of London; the Salvation Army has blossomed into a worldwide ministry today. Although Studd had to live by faith every day for the rest of his life, only eternity will reveal the far-reaching effects of his seemingly illogical gifts.[4]

When God tells you to do something that doesn't make sense to you, trust Him—because it makes sense to Him!

Way of God #3: God wants you to be obedient regardless of the results.

You may obey God and be right in the center of His will when things get worse. If so, start praising God. God is about to reveal Himself to you or do something far beyond what you can imagine. God said to Moses, *Put your hand back into your cloak* (see Exodus 4:7). Moses might have said, "I put my hand in the first time and got leprosy. What will I get the next time?" However, when Moses obeyed, his hand came out restored. If you obey God the first time and it doesn't seem to turn out right, will you have enough faith to do the next thing He tells you? If you don't, you will miss a chance to know God better and see Him work in your life.

My wife, Allison, used the Bible to teach English to international college students at the Chinese church we attended on Sunday mornings. After leading this outreach class for two years, almost all of the students graduated and returned to their home countries. Allison considered disbanding the class, but she believed that God had led her to serve in this capacity, so she remained faithful to prepare lessons even though sometimes no one showed up. In a few months' time, however, four doctors came from China who had never heard the gospel, and they began to diligently attend her class every Sunday, bringing their friends and family.

Likewise, I have prepared to lead Bible studies and no one has shown up. I hollowly reasoned, *If only one person comes, I will be satisfied.* God consoled me: *If you do something unto Me, it's worth it, even if no one else comes.*

When God asks you to do something and it does not turn out like you expected, praise Him because He has something better in mind. As the mother eagle leads the eaglets one phase at a time, God increases our faith one experience at a time so that we will obey Him in any situation.

Way of God #4: God tells you just enough to know what to do next.
Moses had another concern, even though he realized that God was hovering over him: "What if they don't believe these signs?"

Then the LORD said, "If they do not believe you or pay attention to the first miraculous sign, they may believe the second. But if they do not believe these two signs or listen to you, take some water from the Nile and pour it on the dry ground. The water you take from the river will become blood on the ground." (Exodus 4:8-9)

God showed Moses three miracles that he could do in Egypt, but how many plagues did God send upon Egypt? Ten. Why didn't God show all ten to Moses at the beginning? Maybe because Moses wasn't ready to believe God for all He was going to do. God graciously showed him what he could grow to believe. Jesus taught in the parable of the talents that God entrusts us with little things before He allows us to be faithful with bigger tasks (see Matthew 25:14-30).

Danny Akins felt God was telling him to resign from his position on a church staff because he disagreed with the pastor over moral and ethical behavior. Although he had a master of theology degree and was working on his doctorate, he got a menial job paying $5.50 an hour in a real-estate office. One day the owner asked him to clean up a Dumpster that workmen had overrun with their garbage. He had to move the garbage from the overflowing Dumpster to another one. As he worked in the 105-degree weather, he told God, "You are the Lord of the universe, but in this particular case, I'm convinced You have no idea what You're doing." He reminded God of his degrees and experience and ended by saying, "God, it just seems to me that this is a huge waste of my talent and ability. I could be put to better service for the kingdom rather than be throwing garbage from one Dumpster to another."

He sensed God asking, *Danny, what if it is My will for you to be in this Dumpster right now? Would you really want to be somewhere else?*

Danny thought for a long time before answering, "I don't understand. I did the right thing. I acted with moral purity and integrity when I resigned from the church. You know I did. Yet here I am in this garbage. . . . I don't understand it, but yes, I'd much rather be in Your will in a Dumpster than anywhere else in the whole wide world."

God took Danny's humble response to a humiliating situation and eventually made him a seminary president! Danny said, "I really don't want to go through that again, but having been there and having seen what God did, I know that I would not be where I am today if He had not taken me through those experiences."[5]

When you don't understand what God is doing in your life, do what He tells you to do anyway—because He knows the end of the story. He will show you enough to begin and then hover over you and supply *what* is needed *when* it is needed as you learn to trust Him.

Way of God #5: God doesn't want your excuses and is angered by your disobedience and disbelief.
Moses made the excuse that he didn't speak well enough to represent God before Pharaoh.

The LORD said to him, "Who gave man his mouth? Who makes him deaf or mute? Who gives him sight or makes him blind? Is it not I, the LORD? Now go; I will help you speak and will teach you what to say."

But Moses said, "O Lord, please send someone else to do it."

Then the LORD's anger burned against Moses. (Exodus 4:11-14)

It takes a lot to make God angry, but disobedience and unbelief after God has shown you His plan and His power certainly anger Him. God is patient with you when you don't understand why He stirs your nest, but after He hovers over you, shows you His power, and tells you to do something, He expects you to obey. Moses refused. It did not mean that God would not use him, but Moses brought a lot of trouble on himself with his refusal. God substituted Moses' brother, Aaron, as the spokesman, but Aaron became a thorn in Moses' side. It was Aaron who made a golden calf for the people to worship in the wilderness.

Don't pray that God will send someone else if He has told you to go. Don't give God excuses for why you are not capable of doing what He has commanded and empowered you to do. God is trying to get you to grow and believe in His awesome power. That is why He hovers over you when you are sitting on the briars of conviction.

You need an open mind to learn God's ways and an open will to live in God's ways. A stubborn will makes excuses that upset God. I wish we all were sensitive and surrendered to God like Marian, whom I met my freshman year of college. In a New Testament course we had together, we watched a video reenactment of Jesus' crucifixion on Good Friday. Most of the students stared blankly at the video, as if they were overly familiar with what Jesus did on the cross, until Marian started sobbing. This caught their attention. She felt embarrassed afterward yet was baffled at how Christ's death did not affect other believers in the same way. She told me between tears, "I never want to become numb to the cross." That day, I was convicted to keep a sensitive heart that God can freely mold — not a hardened one that He has to break.

WHAT TO DO NEXT

Maybe you're in a situation right now where you're following God, but the circumstances still seem dire. You have begun to doubt that God's ways could really include so much pain for your life, your church, your nation, or your world. You've trusted in God, yet you still have problems. In hard times, the key is to develop a patient, unrelenting faith in God and act on it. You must decide whether you will believe God or just believe the circumstances. Here are three ways to respond positively to God when He stirs your nest and then hovers over you:

1. Rely on God's *power* by focusing on His extraordinary capability to accomplish whatever He desires in your life.
2. Abide in God's *presence* and recognize that the longer the transition of change takes, the more time you will likely spend with Him and the more you can become like Him.
3. Trust the Lord's *purpose* for why He has not yet brought a conclusion to your problems. He has a bigger plan for your life than you do, and you would be wise to place your confidence in Him by following His ways. Solomon instructed,

Trust in the LORD with all your heart
    and lean not on your own understanding;
in all your ways acknowledge him,
    and he will make your paths straight. (Proverbs 3:5-6)

If you are still in the nest getting stuck with the briars and bones, look up. God is on His throne. He is preparing you for the next phase when He spreads His wings and invites you, your church, and your nation to fly with Him.

LET'S GET PERSONAL HERE

1. Which of the five ways that God deals with individuals is most imperative for you to learn in order to respond to God's hovering? Why?
2. How can you apply that "way of God" now?
3. If God gives you a command that you don't understand, what is your best course of action and why? Ignoring it? Studying it? Obeying it? Other?
4. Think of an example from your own life when you obeyed God, but it seemed things didn't turn out right. What did you do next? How can you have enough faith to do the next thing He tells you?
5. If you trust that God is big enough to handle all of your problems, but a difficulty still exists in your life, why do you think God hasn't solved it yet?

PART THREE

TRY YOUR WINGS

Like an eagle that stirs up its nest,
That hovers over its young,
He spread His wings and caught them,
He carried them on His pinions.
The LORD alone guided him,
And there was no foreign god with him.

— DEUTERONOMY 32:11-12, NASB

CHAPTER 5

TRY, TRY AGAIN

*Consider it pure joy, my brothers, whenever you face trials of many
kinds, because you know that the testing of your faith develops
perseverance. Perseverance must finish its work so that you may be
mature and complete, not lacking anything.*

— JAMES 1:2-4

Eagles must, at some point, take that leap outside of their nest for the first time. Unfortunately, since eagles' nests are usually built high in a tree or hundreds of feet above the ground on a cliff, the eagles cannot simply walk out of them.[1] After spending nearly three months in the once-neat nest, the weight from the eaglets and their parents' traffic has flattened and compressed the nest so much that the outer edges slope dangerously downward.[2] This precarious situation makes it increasingly important for the eaglets to try their wings and fly. Yet even after its first flight, the eaglet still has much to learn. It will attempt many new challenges and experience short flights, crash landings, and unsuccessful hunts, but if it continues to press forward and depend on its parents, the eaglet will mature.

The eaglets have always depended on their parents for every need. The difference is that baby eaglets passively depend on their parents for food and protection, whereas now, several months after birth, the maturing eaglets actively participate in the process. I have experienced a similar transition of dependence in my faith in the Lord, from an early faith to an active faith strengthened by years of testing. Childlike faith is simple and uncluttered, but it will not stand the test of the trials and challenges of life if left inactive and undeveloped. God is working in your life not just to get you out of the nest but to teach you to fly.

As we begin this chapter, we are now at the adventuresome young-adult stage of growth in the diagram on page 20, in which we are trying out our faith. You will notice that the numbers on the left side of the diagram show the decreasing responsibility the parent takes and the numbers on the right side show the increasing responsibility the young eagle takes. The shift for initiative is moving rapidly to the young eagle, but the parent is still helping as needed.

In the movie *What About Bob?* Bill Murray has phobias about everything, so he visits a psychiatrist. To keep him from worrying about big things in the future, the doctor encourages him to take baby steps, focusing only on the situation at hand. So he takes half steps out of the office and mumbles to himself, "Baby steps, baby steps through the office, baby steps out the door."[3]

It's easy for us to imagine growth with God as large leaps instead of baby steps. We may think the Israelites just decided in one day to hop over into the Promised Land. Certainly they needed to step over the line, but first they had to walk many steps up to that border. My biggest jump was two miles out of an airplane to the ground! It was heart-stopping and exhilarating, but I first had to step into a tutorial, a skydiving suit, and onto the plane. Eagles must walk from the center of the nest to the edge before they can leap out of it. If you feel like there's currently no major decision in your own life requiring you to dive, don't be embarrassed to take baby steps toward God and the next edge He has for you.

You may feel a lot like the eaglets, which must learn by trial and error, as you enter this process. This chapter is about how you learn to fly by faith through trial and error, which the Bible calls trials, or tests. God wants to develop your faith from experience to experience until you trust Him in every situation. But God does not just leave you alone to learn by experience.

The eaglets' first flying lesson begins with watching their parents flap their wings next to them before flying up above them. Eagles are known for their amazing ability to spiral upward. The rising heat from the earth pushes them higher and higher as they circle above their young until they appear as just a speck in the sky.

The eaglets then try to flap their own wings, imitating the motions of their parents.[4] They progress by jumping from one side of the nest to the other while spreading their wings.[5] Next, they bound up several feet in the air, and some hover on their own above the nest before overcoming their fear of straying too far from it.[6]

As a further enticement, the parent eagle swoops past the nest holding food in its talons. If that doesn't work, the parent will hover directly above the nest dangling a fish just above the eaglets. This hovering excites some eaglets to jump up and out of their nest for a meal—and their first flight.[7]

Moses' song reminds us how God leads us to fly:

Like an eagle that stirs up its nest,
That hovers over its young,
He spread His wings and caught them,
He carried them on His pinions. (Deuteronomy 32:11, NASB)

This echoes what God said in Exodus 19:4: "You yourselves have seen what I did to the Egyptians, and how I bore you on eagles' wings, and brought you to Myself" (NASB). Scientific research supports that a parent eagle can swoop beneath its young that aren't able to fly, catch them on its wings, and take them back up in the sky—all to help them soar. For example, in his book *Life Histories of North American Birds of Prey*, Arthur Cleveland Bent recorded,

We noticed a golden eagle teaching its young one to fly. . . . Roughly handling the young, [the mother] allowed him to drop, I should say, about ninety feet, then she would swoop down under him, wings spread, and he would alight on her back. She would soar to the top of the range with him and repeat the process.[8]

Though popular culture might disagree, the Bible and nature do not contradict each other. Theology and science, however, do not always agree with each other. That is because science is humans' potentially fallible interpretation of nature, while theology is humans' potentially fallible interpretation of God and the Bible. Therefore, scientific passages in Scripture, such as ones about eagles, can be confusing if we misinterpret either our theology or science.

For example, some naturalists and Christians continue to debate whether an eagle carries its young on its wings, as some versions of Deuteronomy 32:11 suggest. This has caused some Bible translators to question whether the pronoun in the last half of the sentence in Deuteronomy 32:11 refers to God or eagles. The New American Standard Bible and some other translations of Deuteronomy 32:11 use "He," indicating that it refers to God, while the *New International Version* and older translations use the neutral pronoun of "its," thus implying that an eagle can carry its young on its feathers. There is no debate, however, that the intent of the verse is that God bears His people on His wings. If eagles can accomplish that feat with their young, then the analogy is supported by all Bible translations. Regardless of whether eagles regularly accomplish this particular feat, God does for His children beyond that which any eagle can do for its own. God took the Israelites from captivity in Egypt to live in the Promised Land. That is His point.

Here is another description of a fledgling's first flight by Frances Hamerstrom, who spent her life studying wildlife:

The . . . eaglet was now alone in the nest. Each time a parent came flying in toward the nest he called for food eagerly; but over and over again, it came with empty feet, and the eaglet grew thinner. He pulled meat scraps from the old dried-up carcasses lying around the nest. . . .

Days passed, and as he lost body fat he became quicker in his movements and paddled ever more lightly when the wind blew, scarcely touching the nest edge; from time to time he was airborne for a moment or two.

Parents often flew past and sometimes fed him. Beating his wings and teetering on the edge of the nest, he screamed for food whenever one flew by. And a parent often flew past just out of reach, carrying delectable meals: a half-grown jack rabbit or a plump rat raided from a dump. . . .

The male eaglet stayed by himself for the most part. He was no longer brooded at night. Hunger and the cold mountain nights were having their effect, not only on his body but on his disposition. A late frost hit the valley, and a night wind ruffled his feathers and chilled his body. When the sunlight reached the eyrie's [a lofty nest's] edge, he sought its warmth; and soon, again, he was bounding in the wind, now light and firm-muscled.

A parent flew by, downwind, dangling a young marmot in its feet. The eaglet almost lost his balance in his eagerness for food. Then the parent swung by again, closer, upwind, and riding the updraft by the eyrie, as though daring him to fly. Lifted light by the wind, he was airborne, flying—or more gliding—for the first time in his life. He sailed across the valley to make a scrambling, almost tumbling landing on a bare knoll. As he turned to get his bearings the parent dropped the young marmot nearby. Half running, half flying he pounced on it, mantled, and ate his fill.[9]

Our friends Rick and Jayne Brekelbaum have watched a local pair of eagles raise their young year after year. Rick said,

I have seen the parent eagles spread their wings in two ways to help the young eagles fly. First, the parent will fly just below while the young eagle "drafts" behind it. The wind from the eagle's wings helps lift it up. At other times the parent eagle flies just above the eaglet, giving it an example of how to soar and drawing it into larger and larger circles.[10]

What a beautiful example of how God spreads His broad wings and takes us where He wants us to go!

The point of Deuteronomy 32:11-12 is that God thrust the people of Israel again and again into situations that required them to risk by faith, He taught them how to trust Him, and He took them out of Egypt on

His wings. An eagle's first authentic flight is an unparalleled experience. After their first landing, some eaglets stand still in shock, sometimes not moving for twenty-four hours.[11] They are dumbfounded at the new environment—after all, they've never seen anything outside their nest.

You, too, will probably experience surprise when you try your wings for the first time. You will be amazed at where God takes you! If you have already taken that first flight, you will agree that the end result of following God is priceless, but the path to successful soaring is rarely painless or flawless. As you begin to fly for the first time or begin a new adventure of faith, you will likely experience frustrations and a feeling of inability, but God will patiently develop your faith to match His supply.

Moses asked the Israelites,

Has any god ever tried to take for himself one nation out of another nation, by testings [God's stirring the nest], by miraculous signs and wonders [God's powerful hovering] . . . like all the things the LORD your God did for you in Egypt before your very eyes [God's leading them to fly]? (Deuteronomy 4:34)

He showed them these things so they might know that the Lord is God and so they would obey Him and grow in faith in Him.

WHAT IF I FALL?

Though eaglets begin by hopping and flapping within the nest, on their first flight outside of the nest, about half of them fall short.[12] While that statistic sounds frightening, keep in mind that the percentage of eaglets that survive if they never leave the nest is zero! Although by instinct the eaglets sense they should fly, flying is a skill learned through trial and error. If you want a mature faith, admit that it's okay to fail, but also trust that God will lift you up when you fall.

A colleague of our oldest son, Randy (Matt's dad), lost $3 million on one of his projects while working for a major computer company. When his boss called him into his office, the employee presented his written resignation. "What's this?" his boss asked. Randy's colleague told him that he was resigning because he had failed. The boss handed the resignation back to him and said, "Do you think we are going to let you go when we just invested $3 million in your education?" Thankfully God doesn't give up on us when we fail but puts us in another situation where we can try again.

IF AT FIRST YOU DON'T SUCCEED . . .

Even eaglets that are successful at flying still experience trial and error. Their flights are short and their landings tumultuous—slamming into the ground and tumbling.[13] One eaglet's first flight ended with it crashing into a tree and hanging upside down, holding onto a limb with one foot before falling to the ground.[14]

If an eaglet falls, it hops up and attempts to fly again.[15] As the eagle presses on, its flight capability increases fifty to one hundred yards with each new flight.[16] Maybe you've tried to follow God outside of your nest before, gotten bruised, and are tempted to quit trying. Don't give up on God; He hasn't given up on you. Everyone who follows God must endure challenges and mistakes in order to grow. No one but God is perfect, and He is patient and merciful with you as He leads you to maturity. Similarly, you will grow significantly in faith each time you try your wings.

If you want to learn to fly, messing up is inevitable, but giving up is unacceptable. Charles Goodyear saw an india-rubber life preserver and was captivated by its potential. But there seemed to be one insurmountable barrier—weather constantly hardened or melted it. He committed his life to solving the problem. He tried thousands of experiments, spent all of his money, and was ridiculed by society, who labeled him insane. However, he endured the trials and solved the problem.[17] Thanks to him, your car can ride smoothly on rubber tires.

Theodor Geisel, better known as Dr. Seuss, had his first book rejected by twenty-three publishers before Random House published it. If he had given up, you would not know about *The Cat in the Hat* and *Green Eggs and Ham*.[18]

Are you in the midst of trying and failing? Don't let failure keep you from ultimate victory.

STARVING TO LEARN

Once you leave the nest, you need your heavenly Father just as much as you did earlier. In the same way, the eaglets must continue to depend on their parents for flight training and hunting for meals. Initially, an eaglet may catch its prey in only one of eighteen attempts.[19] Eagles do not reach maturity until they learn to fly and forage successfully for food, as their parents do. If the eaglets succeed in flight, the parent will deliver food to the young eagles where they land. For the next three months, every single day the eaglet will fly after its parent as much as its young wings can handle, and the parent will continue to feed it as it progresses.[20]

One or two sin areas typically test you more than other vices throughout your life. I have seen it in my own life, and you can observe how Abraham's grandson Jacob was tested by deceit a lot in his life. He struggled with his older brother, Esau, and tricked their dad to get the blessing for himself. He struggled with Laban over working long enough to marry his daughter. Laban tricked him into working fourteen years instead of seven to marry Rachel. Later Jacob wrestled with God — literally, as a man. God showed His power as He injured Jacob's hip, reminding Jacob to worship Him. Jacob wrestled with God, and God gave him the name Israel, which means "he struggles with God" (see Genesis 32:28). The name Israel can also be defined as "prince with God, he strives with God, let God rule, or God strives."[21] The descendants of Jacob were also collectively known as Israel, and they strove with God for good and bad. When you are tested, take the advice of one of the interpretations of Israel's name: Let God rule.

GROWING THROUGH TESTING

God fed the Israelites as He led them out of their Egyptian nest and into flight school in the wilderness. Just before the Israelites entered the Promised Land, Moses said to them,

> Remember how the LORD your God led you all the way in the desert these forty years, to humble you and to test you in order

to know what was in your heart, whether or not you would keep his commands. He humbled you, causing you to hunger and then feeding you with manna, which neither you nor your fathers had known, to teach you that man does not live on bread alone but on every word that comes from the mouth of the LORD. Your clothes did not wear out and your feet did not swell during these forty years. Know then in your heart that as a man disciplines his son, so the LORD your God disciplines you. (Deuteronomy 8:2-5)

God tests you in the same ways for the same reasons. First, He tests you to humble you. You can't grow if you are proud and think your way is the best way. The first lesson you must learn is how great He is and how weak you are. He humbled the people of Israel by supplying manna from heaven, which they had to collect every day, thereby acknowledging that they were totally dependent on Him for every bite they ate. Have you already developed an active dependence on God for every day's needs, or are you tempted to just do things on your own?

Second, He tests you to reveal what is in your heart and whether or not you will keep His commandments. You know someone's heart by observing his or her actions. When you face your next trial, imagine a loud voice from heaven, like the one that pops up on television, saying, "This is a test!"

Third, He demonstrates that your soul starves apart from Him. Jesus quoted Deuteronomy 8:3 — "Man does not live on bread alone but on every word that comes from the mouth of the LORD" — to Satan when He fasted forty days in the wilderness, proving that God's Word alone could sustain Him to fulfill the Father's purpose for His life. How many consecutive days have you gone without eating? How many consecutive days have you ever spent without devouring God's provision of the Bread of Life?

Lastly, God tests you because His goal for you is a mature faith (see James 1:2-4 at the beginning of this chapter, on page 77).

When God called me to go to seminary, He tested my faith to see how actively I would depend on Him. I remembered Abraham's call and felt that God was telling Shirley and me to leave where we were living and move to Fort Worth, Texas. Several friends who were already at seminary cautioned me, "There are so many preachers at this seminary that I haven't even had an opportunity to preach in two years, let alone pastor." I said, "Well, I'm willing to preach on the streets or in the jails." Shirley and I had to face the reality that we had no church in which to serve, no job to support us, and our first baby was on the way.

When we left the church where I had been pastor, they gave us a "pounding"—everyone brought food and other things we might need. Since many of the members were on welfare, we got a lot of welfare commodities, especially pinto beans. I said, "Let's put the beans back for a rainy day so we'll have something to eat if we run out of money." Every time the funds ran low that first semester, Shirley would get ready to cook some of the beans, and then money would come from an unexpected source. God provided opportunities for me to preach more than ever—and we ate well! We started a church the second semester, and through it all God kept His promise. In fact, we never ate all the beans! I saved a jar of them to show our future children and grandchildren that God is faithful to do all you ask when you trust and follow Him.

GOD REPLACES LOST FEATHERS

The testing or difficulty you may experience while growing in faith may include the loss of relationships or possessions. An eagle loses its tattered feathers at least once a year, but new feathers replace them.[22] This renewing of feathers is what David referred to when he said that "your youth is renewed like the eagle's" as you grow closer to God (Psalm 103:5). Eagles have seven thousand feathers, but their combined weight is a mere twenty-one ounces. If you held thirty eagle feathers in your hand, they would weigh less than one penny. God has given you many feathers—unique experiences, talents, and spiritual gifts—that may not seem to weigh much, but collectively they equip you for a huge assignment from God. At times you may endure a loss of some of these feathers that you thought you needed to do God's will. But remember that He is willing and able to replace anything that you give up for Him with something new and better.

Our youngest daughter, her husband, and their three children experienced many ups and downs as God replaced their feathers. They sold their household goods and cars to go to another country to serve the Lord. I could see in Krista's eyes and hear in her voice how difficult it was for them to leave their family, friends, church, and home. They shared the journal of their six-year-old daughter, Amber, with me:

I am sad. olmost evrething in my hose is gone. the coch the bed my dog my toys. all my brothr baby stof is gone. my mom and Dad have to sleep on an ear mattres. my bother has to sleep in a plac en play. me and my sister have to sleep on the flor.

As they grieved their losses, I reminded them what Jesus told His disciples: "And everyone who has left houses or brothers or sisters or father or mother or children or fields for my sake will receive a hundred times as much and will inherit eternal life" (Matthew 19:29). Our son-in-law responded, "I never paid much attention to what He said about leaving your wife or brothers or parents or children until now." Despite the sacrifice required, they responded in obedience to what they sensed God was leading them to do. Three years later in that faraway country, Amber, now nine, wrote this song:

The Lord Has Come
I think how great the Lord is to me.
He has come to save.
I think of the Lord and remember what He has done for me.
Nothing is impossible for Him.
The Lord has come!

God gives a new song to those who follow Him through trials. God may be initiating a change that requires you to leave where you are before He shows you where to go next. That does not mean you should quit your job tomorrow, but you need to come to the point where you are willing to do anything God requires. He promises He will go with you and bless you.

Growing Through a Crisis of Belief

After experiencing trials and sorrow as you follow God, you will come to a turning point and have to decide whether or not you are going to press forward. In the midst of difficult circumstances, there comes a point when you must either believe—and enter a new level of trust and dependency on the Father—or choose not to believe. This is what we call a crisis of belief. The situation challenges you to trust God in an unprecedented manner and grow or else stunt your growth by doubting God. If you turn back at the point of uncertainty, adverse circumstances, or risk, you will miss the blessings of God. In this case, you cannot remain both comfortable and committed. God's blessings come outside of your comfort zone.

Brian and I became friends when we were in high school and attended the same church youth group. He wasn't the typical church kid. He came from a rough background with influences from gangs and drugs. He had a radical salvation experience—every salvation is radical, but Brian lived out the radical implications of salvation. He was excited to receive God's grace and grow in it. He wrote Christian raps. He created Christian artwork that resembled graffiti. He was a relevant witness and fun to be around.

I ran into Brian again five years after high school. The tattoos on his body summed up his past ten years. On his right arm and the right side of his chest, Brian had tattoos representing God and the city we grew up in. On his left side were tattoos symbolizing death. Since high school, he had served in the war in Iraq and, back in the United States, had moved to a city that he felt was spiritually suffocating him. He had returned to drugs and other things he wasn't proud of. He was at a crisis of belief with God, but he knew his life needed to change.

Salvation is certainly a crisis of belief for a person, but it is not an isolated point in time. You cannot believe God for salvation and expect to coast from that point forward.

When your first attempt at something new is unsuccessful, you're likely to be tempted to give up and return to what is familiar. After their first flights, some eaglets return to their nest after failing to hunt independently.[23] They know they can get a good meal back home. Some eaglets remain close to their home nest for nearly two years.[24] The parents may accept the eaglets back temporarily, but eagles will eventually drive their children away from the nest.[25] Some human parents can identify with them!

The Israelites felt like those eaglets several times in the wilderness. After having faith to follow God outside of their four-hundred-year-old nest in Egypt, some Israelites came to a crisis of belief, questioning if God's path was worth the pain. They struggled to trust that God was leading them to a much better place. They wanted to make a U-turn back to Egypt. To prevent them from returning to Egypt and reverting to their old lifestyle, God chose not to lead Israel on the shortest path from Egypt to the Promised Land (see Exodus 13:17). He intentionally led them into the middle of nowhere, where they had to be totally dependent on Him. In the wilderness, God gradually transformed Israel's dependence into faith.

Unfortunately, the first time the Israelites arrived at the border of the Promised Land, they failed the test of faith. That time, the Israelites' crisis of belief was whether they could trust God to overthrow the mighty people living in Canaan. Most of them lost heart, and as a result, they spent almost two generations wandering in the wilderness.

God wasn't done with the Israelites though. He picked them up and helped them enter the Promised Land forty years later. It is interesting that the two things the unfaithful spies cited as reasons for *not* taking the Promised Land were the first two things God enabled the faithful spies, Joshua and Caleb, to conquer—fortified cities and giants (see Numbers 13:28). Joshua led them to conquer Jericho by the very bizarre but God-ordained method of marching around the city until the walls fell down (see Joshua 6:1-27). Caleb said, "I'll take the hill country where the giants live!" (see Joshua 14:6-15), and God gave him the land for his faithfulness. Forty-five years after he received God's promise, Caleb was prosperous and "the land had rest from war" (Joshua 14:15).

The second time around, the Israelites placed their faith in God and began living in the land as He had promised Abraham. Whenever you spread your wings of faith, God will reward you, just as He plentifully blessed Israel when they finally took flight.

No Turning Back

When I was a young pastor, I experienced a crisis of belief regarding a short-term missions opportunity. The International Mission Board was enlisting six hundred pastors, musicians, and laypersons to be leaders on a three-week missions trip to Japan and Hong Kong—but I wasn't among those chosen initially. One night I could not sleep because of my strong desire to go, and I vividly remember sitting in my recliner around three in the morning asking God why I wasn't chosen to go since I was the one who was going to be a missionary.

It should have been obvious to me why I wasn't going. I was not one of the two hundred well-known pastors out of some four thousand churches who received an invitation. In addition, I didn't have the money. The cost of the ticket was $1,500—equal to almost four months of my salary. Nevertheless, I challenged God by asking Him why I couldn't go.

God responded, *Because you don't have the faith.*

"If that is all it takes," I said, "I'll have the faith."

Eventually I did receive the invitation to go to Japan, so I shared the opportunity with our church along with my conviction that I was supposed to go. They began to collect an offering that grew to about $500. It stayed at that level for several weeks. I discovered later that some members were boycotting the offering because they said their pastor should stay home and visit the sick and preach their funerals if they were to die.

Finally, the sponsors of the missions trip called and asked, "Are you going or not? We have to know today." At that moment I had a crisis of belief. Should I answer based on my obvious lack of money, or should I maintain the faith that I told God I would have? I shot up a quick prayer, took a deep breath, and resolutely answered, "Yes, I am going. Count me in." Saying that out loud helped, but I still didn't know how I would get the money.

The next Sunday I told the congregation the situation and invited them to give for the last time. I preached about God telling the Israelites to go take the Promised Land. We took the regular offering at the end of the service, but before anyone could count the money, one of the ushers came to the front and said, "Brother Avery, you are on your way to Japan!"

"How's that?" I answered.

"Several of us men have agreed to go to the bank and borrow the money to send you."

I replied, "Thank you, Joe, and the others of you who have made this offer, but I don't believe that is the way God wants to answer my prayer. I believe that enough money has already been given in the offering to cover the cost of the trip."

After the service I went home and ate lunch while the tellers counted the money. In the middle of lunch the phone rang. "Brother Avery, guess how much the offering is for the trip."

I answered, "$1,500!"

He shot back, "$1,503.43," and laughed. "The $3.43 is for coffee money!"

I cannot tell you how much that built my faith! Two other men from our church and I helped lead more than six hundred people to Christ on that trip, and the impact on our church was life-changing. Over the next several years, eight families from our church went overseas as career missionaries.

Almost forty years later, while I was serving with the International Mission Board, we experienced a greater growth in prospective missionaries than in gifts to send them. Almost half of our budget came from the annual Lottie Moon Christmas Offering for global missions. Although we had seen incremental growth, we had not met our goal for more than ten years. We needed to receive an increase of $20 million to send the missionaries who were ready to go. As I replayed in my mind the experience of my first missions trip, I told others, "I believe that God is going to cause His people to respond and give a record offering." It took a more mature faith to believe God for $20 *million* than for $1,500, but it was the same kind of faith in God during a crisis of belief. The result was an increase in the offering by more than $21 million—18.4 percent more than was given the previous year. We were able to send all the missionaries who had been waiting to go.

I am naturally a frugal person. Growing up, I picked up coins off the sidewalk. When spring rolled around, my brother Kyle and I sold candy bars. I washed cars in the summer, raked the neighbors' leaves in the fall, and shoveled sidewalks in the winter.

When I was in high school, I felt that God wanted me to serve Him by going to Turkey for a month. It would be my first international mission. I had no clue, however, how I would raise the $3,000. Although I was proactive in raising money, I thought other people would be more than glad to dump the money on me! Two weeks before the deadline, I still needed to raise more than $1,000, and I wondered, *Did God really call me to go on this trip?* I believed the answer was yes, but my youth pastor, John Fream, rightfully admonished me that faith without works is no faith at all (see James 2:17). I became willing to use my own savings for the Turkey trip, but I continued to talk to even more people about the trip. God enabled me to meet my deadline, and that trip jump-started me for the journey I am still on.

I raised support to participate in four missions trips over the next five years before coordinating the Avery T. Willis Center for Global Outreach at my alma mater. In my first year, the university sponsored and organized eleven American and international missions trips. Each of the students had to raise the funds necessary for his or her own trip — the budgets totaled more than $150,000. I personally didn't raise that much money, but I certainly prayed fervently that God would provide it all so that the students could serve Him around the world. Trusting God for my first international assignment to Turkey enabled me to trust Him for fifty times more money five years later. Just imagine how much less I would have believed in the possibility had I not followed Him through the first crisis of belief.

Learning to live by faith is not just cranking up your courage, gritting your teeth, and trying to do better. It is a time when you totally trust the Lord to do what you cannot do. Yet a crisis of belief also challenges you to act on what you really believe and leave the results to God. Though both faith and actions are important, to merely believe is simpler than *living* what you believe. When you act on faith, it causes you to truly trust God.

Acting on faith is hard, uncomfortable, and often painful; however, it's worth it because that is how you learn to soar.

LET'S GET PERSONAL HERE

1. Remember a crisis of belief that you faced in the past and how you responded to it. If you are experiencing a crisis of belief now, tell God what you are struggling to trust Him for.
2. What changes, if any, should you make in how you experience God through the Bible and prayer?
3. Do you realize that before God can catch you on His wings (see Deuteronomy 32:11), you need to be out of the nest and in the air? What do you need to do to get airborne?
4. Describe some risks you will have to take to fly with God.
5. How safe does God want you to be? Is the center of God's will really the safest place to be?

CHAPTER 6

GROWING YOUR FAITH THROUGH A WORD FROM GOD

So then faith comes by hearing, and hearing by the word of God.
— ROMANS 10:17, NKJV

When you experience a crisis of belief, how will you grow in your faith? Moses gave us the answer, and Jesus quoted it: "Man does not live on bread alone but on *every word that comes from the mouth of the LORD*" (Deuteronomy 8:3, emphasis mine). As the eaglets live on the food their parents bring or they hunt themselves, so we live and grow by the Word of God. Hebrews 11:1 says, "Faith is being sure of what we hope for and certain of what we do not see." *Hoping so* is quite different from *being certain*. Faith is more than hope; it is based on certainty because of what God says. Your faith grows when you believe and act upon the promises of God in His Word. Romans 10:17 shows us that faith comes from hearing the Word of God, believing what God says in the message, and then staking one's life on it.

A word from God is His way to develop your growing faith. Getting a word from God means that the Holy Spirit reveals a specific scripture to you in your situation and impresses you to claim it and act on it by faith. It may be a promise, a warning, a prohibition, a rebuke, a correction, or an instruction. In other words, God speaks personally to you through His Word and its application to your situation, and He challenges you to believe Him.

Paul encouraged Timothy that "all Scripture is God-breathed and is useful for teaching, rebuking, correcting and training in righteousness" (2 Timothy 3:16). All Scripture has worth even if you don't have a personal connection with each verse. For example, even though the book of Numbers is full of censuses and genealogies, it's still worth studying and applying. Every part of the Bible is the Word of God; furthermore, because it is alive (see Hebrews 4:12), God may apply any part of His Word to contemporary issues in your life.

My first conscious memory of getting a word from God for a specific occasion was when I was a college freshman and a chapel speaker challenged us to give sacrificially to the Lottie Moon Christmas Offering for global missions. He talked about students who had gone without food in order to give and one lady who had given her wedding ring for this missions offering. I wanted to give, but I had no extra money. I was trying to help pay for my tuition by working twenty hours a week while carrying a full load of courses.

As I prayed about how I should give sacrificially during the following year, I sensed that God wanted me to give an extra 10 percent to missions above my regular tithe. God gave me a word—Matthew 6:33, which says, "But seek first his kingdom and his righteousness, and all these things will be given to you as well." I really believed that since I was seeking God's righteousness and His kingdom, He would supply all my physical needs just as the verse promised. Every week I put the extra 10 percent in a Christmas Club bank account specifically so that I could give a worthy offering to missions the next Christmas season when it was collected.

In the midst of my perceived sacrifice, God began to provide for me in unexpected ways. When a professor gave me a suit and some other clothes, I told my roommate, "I just can't out-give God. I think I am giving sacrificially, and He gives me back more than I gave. I am using a spoon, and He is using a shovel!" My faith began to grow on the basis of believing that promise from God's Word. For the rest of my life, He has faithfully cared for my needs because I put Him and His kingdom first.

The strongest word from God I've ever received was when I was praying about an opportunity to revisit Asia. I went there for the first time as a freshman in college and got to know my teaching partner, Allison, while we ministered there. We began dating after the trip. When someone invited me to return to Asia the following summer to share Jesus for two months while backpacking, Allison and I were already seriously dating; the thought of being separated for two months made my decision harder.

The most important factor in my decision was what God wanted me to do. I prayed and prayed, but it wasn't until God spoke to me through the Bible that I knew He wanted me to go to this country for a second time. I read Genesis 28:15, which says, "I am with you and will watch over you wherever you go, and I will bring you back to this land. I will not leave you until I have done what I have promised you." God originally spoke that promise to Jacob in a dream of a stairway to heaven, but that day I felt like God was speaking directly to my heart as well. I memorized the promise from God and worshipfully recited it during my flight halfway around the globe. My new environments on the trip occasionally made me scared, confused, uncomfortable, or homesick, yet I increasingly trusted God because of the promise He gave me in His Word.

That doesn't mean that I've never made the mistake of trying to do something apart from a word from God. Also during my freshman year in college, the campus experienced a spiritual awakening. Three friends and I decided that we should get a tent and go from town to town throughout Oklahoma and conduct what we called revivals—preaching campaigns that we hoped would bring true spiritual revival like we had experienced. We sought a tent from every source possible and waited daily with anticipation that one would materialize. We were sure that God was going to use us as little Billy Grahams that summer. Our zeal surpassed our wisdom. We had not even thought about enlisting the churches in those towns to sponsor the meetings. Ultimately, we did not get a tent or conduct meetings.

Later in the summer we tried to conduct a citywide crusade in Borger, Texas, where one of my buddies lived. We secured the high school auditorium, painted billboards, and advertised with posters and spots on the radio. The week we were to start the crusade, a local pastor called us in and reprimanded us for not engaging the churches in developing a local organization of churches to sponsor the meetings. He told us that he, along with others, had put pressure on the school superintendent to withdraw the offer of the high-school auditorium.

I said, "God, You can't let them stop us. Look how much we have done. We will be so ashamed." Although we tried other venues, eventually we slipped out of town the day the crusade was to begin. It was a hard lesson. We were enthusiastic and visionary, but we did not base our actions on a promise from God; instead we trusted our own ingenuity and hard work. I learned through that experience that every attempt at faith should be grounded in a promise from God that is initiated by Him. I have also learned that not all of God's promises are fulfilled immediately. I still have some Bible promises that I believe God will fulfill in the future.

FLIGHTS OF FAITH

As you try out your own spiritual wings, how do you progress beyond disappointments and mistakes? Let me suggest some guidelines for spreading your wings of faith so that God can accomplish His purpose for you:

How to Build a Dynamic Faith
1. Scriptural authority
2. Holy Spirit's verification
3. Alignment with God's purposes
4. A God-given opportunity or challenge
5. Spiritual markers
6. Godly counsel

Start with Scriptural Authority
Faith is based on a clear word from God. Moses received a word from God at the burning bush that he would be successful. God said, "I will be with you. And this will be the sign to you that it is I who have sent you: When you have brought the people out of Egypt, you will worship God on this mountain" (Exodus 3:12). No doubt that word from God sustained Moses until he brought the Israelites to Mount Sinai.

You may not hear a voice from God like Moses did. How can you test whether you have a word from God for a specific situation? First, if God impresses on you a scripture that is a clear promise that any believer could claim, you can be confident in acting in faith on it. My first faith attempt based on Matthew 6:33 (when I sacrificially gave money to missions in college) was this kind of promise.

Second, you can claim a word from God when a biblical situation or example matches your situation and you are impressed to ask God in faith to do the same for you. I did that in the example in the last chapter, when I preached on a parallel situation of entering a new country before we took the offering to go to Japan for my first missions trip.

Third, God may lead you to take a principle that can be applied in your context even though it is different from the scriptural context. It is not as certain as the previous two, but the Holy Spirit has the right to take a passage and apply it within the context of your life.

But how do you get a word from God if you are not spending time in His Word? I didn't begin to understand personal worship until I entered college and read a tract from The Navigators, *Seven Minutes with God*, which said anyone could take seven minutes each day for Bible reading and prayer. I said, "I can take seven minutes even if I get up late!" A strange thing happened in the process—I met God! After that, I was not trying to establish a spiritual discipline but to nurture a relationship. I began to get up earlier and earlier because I wanted to spend more time with God. No one has ever become a mature disciple who does not spend time in God's Word and apply it to his or her daily life. Most of my Bible promises come out of my daily reading of God's Word rather than my consciously looking for them.

Look for the Holy Spirit's Verification

Anytime you get a word from God, you need the Holy Spirit to apply the passage to your life. Instead of looking for a scripture that confirms what you want to do, allow the Holy Spirit to confirm in your heart that a specific scripture is for you. Most of my words from God jump off the page at me during my regular reading and study of God's Word as the Holy Spirit illuminates them to me.

In anticipation that God is going to speak to me through His Word about the things I face, I keep a running list of what I need to hear from

Him about. After all these years I am still amazed how He takes my regular daily Bible reading and applies it to my present situation and list of problems through the Spirit's affirmation. The Holy Spirit's work is to show you whether or not the application that you are considering is from God. If your impression really is from God, the Holy Spirit will continue to affirm over time that you need to apply the scripture to your situation and act on it. Jesus explained this phenomenon like this:

> The Spirit of truth . . . will guide you into all truth. He will not speak on his own; he will speak only what he hears, and he will tell you what is yet to come. He will bring glory to me by taking from what is mine and making it known to you. All that belongs to the Father is mine. That is why I said the Spirit will take from what is mine and make it known to you. (John 16:13-15)

I believe memorizing Scripture improves our receptivity in hearing from God because Jesus promised that the Holy Spirit "will remind you of everything I have said to you" (John 14:26). How can you be reminded of something you've never learned? To memorize the Bible for the long term, I suggest that you utilize a tool such as the Topical Memory System, which can be found at www.navpress.com.

I once asked God questions about dating and how I would know that I had found the spouse He intended for me. The Holy Spirit reminded me of Philippians 4:6-8, which I had memorized. As I recited verses 6 and 7, He told me that if I would be patient and prayerful, He'd give me peace about finding "the one." I had never heard those verses applied to dating or marriage, and I thanked God for perfectly answering my questions. However, I still had a question about what my standards for a wife should be. I was afraid that I was seeking a perfect person as a spouse; perhaps I needed to lower my standards. Then God reminded me of verse 8: "Finally, brothers, whatever is true, whatever is noble, whatever is right, whatever is pure, whatever is lovely, whatever is admirable—if anything is excellent or praiseworthy—think about such things." He told me, *If you can think on these things, a person can be these things. These are to be your standards for your own life and for a wife.* That verse can relate to so many situations, yet God specifically applied it to my question.

Amazingly, a few months later I met my future wife, Allison. In our first conversation about dating, before I told her about my Philippians experience, Allison mentioned that God had recently spoken Philippians 4:8 to her as a promise about her future spouse. That word from God, along with the several other factors described in this chapter, led us on the wonderful path toward marriage.

Align with God's Purposes

In addition to having biblical authority and the Holy Spirit's counsel, you should check your interpretation to see how it lines up with God's purposes throughout His Word. For example, Moses told the Israelites that God had sent him to lead them out of Egypt and into the Promised Land. They could have rejected Moses' leadership by protesting that Egypt was one of the most powerful nations on earth. However, God had told them His purpose four hundred years earlier when He said to their forefather, Abraham,

> Know for certain that your descendents will be strangers in a country not their own, and they will be enslaved and mistreated four hundred years. But I will punish the nation they serve as slaves, and afterward they will come out with great possessions. . . . [And] your descendents will come back here. (Genesis 15:13-16)

Earlier I told you that I felt God leading me to resign my weekend pastorate after I graduated from college and move to Fort Worth, Texas, to enter seminary. I had no prospect for income but felt sure God had called me. I sensed God was calling me, as He did Abraham, to go to "another land" where He would bless Him. The purpose God gave Abraham was the same as my purpose—to bless the peoples of the world. I was convinced that God's call was in line with His overall purpose.

Test whether you are applying a correct interpretation of the passage in the context of the whole Scripture because God will not lead you to do anything that is contrary to His stated purpose and mission. The Scripture will also clarify how you can fulfill God's purpose in your particular situation. For example, God said we are to love all races. If your plans discount or mistreat a person of another race, you can be sure you are not in line with God's purpose.

Additionally, you can't claim scriptural authority for something that is forbidden in the Scriptures, such as asking God to give you someone else's spouse (as one person I know tried!). Familiarize yourself with these biblical themes so that you don't split hairs over minor points: God does what is best, God brings life out of death, God wants a relationship with all people, God forgives repentant sinners and punishes unrepentant sinners, God expects obedience and justice from us, God makes and keeps covenants, God shows grace and love.

Evaluate Whether an Opportunity or Challenge Is God-Given

The first three guidelines are more objective than interpreting whether or not God sent a particular circumstance. A circumstance could be used to prove anything if taken alone. When God is leading you, however, He often allows circumstances to enter your life that seem to have His fingerprints on them. Prayer and sensitivity to the Spirit during a series of occurrences should substantiate whether the circumstances are providential or coincidental.

Monica Skiles was preparing to go to Tanzania as a two-year missionary. One day, she and a group of other missionaries who were training in Virginia received four assignments to complete in three hours in nearby Washington, D.C. They were to observe internationals, engage them in conversation, eat some international food, and bring someone closer to Jesus. After two hours, Monica was panicking.

"Lord," she prayed, "I need Your help. I've seen internationals, and I've eaten their food—but I haven't really talked to any of them, and I certainly haven't brought anyone closer to Jesus. I need You to confirm to me that You really want me to go to Tanzania." She said amen and looked down the corridor where a display of African arts and crafts was being exhibited.

Monica picked up a handcrafted item.

"It's from Tanzania," the merchant said.

"Oh? I'm moving to Tanzania," Monica said.

"Where will you be living?" the woman asked.

"In Dar es Salaam."

"I am from Dar es Salaam. What will you be doing?"

"I will be teaching kindergarten in the Haven of Peace Academy," Monica replied.

"My granddaughters go to that school," the woman said. "My granddaughters have come home telling me about Jesus. They said He loves me and that if I should ever get in trouble, I should call on Him and He will hear me."

When Monica left the station an hour later, she had prayed with the woman and now carried in her pocket two letters to the woman's grandchildren. As it turned out, one of the woman's granddaughters was a student in her class when she arrived in Dar es Salaam![1]

Sometimes you are presented with an opportunity that seems to line up with the direction in which God has been guiding you, and He uses that opportunity to confirm His leading to you. Although you should never take circumstances alone, when they corroborate with God's leading in the first three guidelines, circumstances can give you a sense of destiny and cause you to step out in faith.

Use Your Spiritual Markers as a Compass

A spiritual marker is a time when you knew that you experienced God and saw Him work in your life. God gives you spiritual markers so you can see how He has worked mightily in your life. Often you will look back at your spiritual markers and see how God has been preparing you for this very opportunity. Why don't you stop now and jot down your spiritual markers so that you can see what God has been doing in your life? Share them with your family so that they can know their heritage and receive direction for the future.

Although God's leadings in the past may not look exactly like your present situation, He did not make a mistake when He led you then. He will help you see how the challenge you face now is in line with past directions. I have been asked to do many good things that I turned down because they did not line up with my spiritual markers. I always go back to what I know God has said to me in the past and see how that lines up with a new opportunity. The more spiritual markers you have, the more accurately you can discern whether you should take a new direction. That does not mean that God does not lead you in different directions at times, but His leading will not violate how He has led you in the past.

Test Your Interpretation Through Godly Counsel

God has put you in a church body for a reason. You need counsel from other believers to help you see things from a different perspective. Seek out people who display the fruits of a close walk with God and share with them what you think God is asking you to believe and do. Sometimes they will bring up a point that you have not considered. At other times they will resonate with what you are sensing. Evaluate whether they are just trying to agree with you or if they have a real sense that God is leading in this direction. Not all godly people will have the same counsel, so it is wise to ask multiple believers whom you trust.

You can learn God's ways from His Word, from experience, and from other people. I'd encourage you to learn from all three sources, though the last two should be rooted in the Bible. I think that other believers are an underutilized resource for understanding God's ways. Always have a mentor — a mature Christian who knows the ways of God — and someone you are mentoring — a "Timothy," the young man the apostle Paul discipled.

When I was in high school, Avery took me with him to Cuba, where he was discipling local ministers. As we traveled, I remember asking him several theological questions that I didn't understand from my personal Bible reading. When I began preaching and teaching on Sundays at age nineteen, I sought out my first long-term mentor, Leroy Hogue. I was hearing only *myself* preach and needed to hear the wisdom that this retired missionary offered to me for a full afternoon each week. Many people have mentored me — from laymen to pastors to family and friends. Several simultaneous mentors are wonderful, but make sure that you are having an individual, intentional, and consistent time with at least one person who exemplifies and teaches God's ways.

After you have received counsel from individuals regarding an important decision, you might want to ask your church or its leaders to give you their counsel. When you have asked enough godly people and you are getting similar answers, take their counsel back to the Lord. Go through the whole process of these guidelines again in prayer to evaluate whether God is confirming the decision or modifying it. In the final analysis, *you* are responsible for how you understand and follow God's leadership.

DARE TO FLY

After you have examined these guidelines, you may discover that God is calling you to something unprecedented. God wants to demonstrate His powerful purposes in your life; it is time to get out of the nest and fly! It is scary, but you will sense in your heart that this is a sacred moment. When you leap into the air, you will sense the wind of the Spirit beneath your wings of faith.

I watched people paragliding off mountains in Switzerland and New Zealand without the slightest thought of doing it myself. I thought it was crazy. But over the years as I continued watching, the desire to join them mounted up in my soul. With a paraglider, you actually fly like a bird soaring upward on currents of air by means of an elongated parachute swaying above you.

Finally I made up my mind to jump the next chance I had, and while in the Julian Alps in Slovenia, the opportunity came. As I looked down thousands of feet to the lake and valley below, I began to question my sanity. My copilot threw some grass in the air and said, "Not good. But when I say go, run," nodding his head vigorously. Without further ado, he jumped into his harness, and we ran right off the cliff! We plummeted probably a hundred feet in a free fall that took my breath away. Then the parachute caught the wind and jerked us upward. It was so wonderful to fly like a bird in ever-expanding circles between the mountains. As we glided in that peaceful silence over a lake, with only the rush of the wind on our cheeks, I worshipped God with the world lying at our feet. My first impression was, *Why have I never done this before? What I have missed!*

Time and time again God has led me to launch out once again in faith. Every time I do so, I get butterflies and feel like I did during the first hundred feet of the paraglide. But I know the parachute of God's Word is sure to keep me soaring.

YOUR CHALLENGE

What is God challenging you to believe now as the next step in building your faith? It will certainly stretch you to believe God for more than you can do or perhaps even imagine. Reflect on the following word from God and ask what you should believe Him for in your present situation: "Now to him who is able to do immeasurably more than all we ask or imagine, according to his power that is at work within us, to him be glory in the church and in Christ Jesus throughout all generations, for ever and ever! Amen" (Ephesians 3:20-21). No matter how good your imagination is, God has a much bigger vision for your life than you do.

LET'S GET PERSONAL HERE

1. Think about how the Lord has grown your faith through a specific verse in the Bible. What scripture has the Holy Spirit recently laid on your heart that speaks to a situation you are facing?
2. How can you test whether you have a word from God for a specific situation?
3. What other confirmations from circumstances or godly counsel are you receiving for your situation?
4. Which of the six guidelines is the most challenging to you? Why? What do you think you should do next?
5. Make a list of your past spiritual markers. Do you see a trend? What has God been doing in your life? What is God challenging you to believe now as the next step in building your faith?

PART FOUR

SOAR WITH GOD

Like an eagle . . . the LORD alone guided him,
And there was no foreign god with him.
He made him ride on the high places of the earth,
And he ate the produce of the field.

— DEUTERONOMY 32:11-13, NASB

CHAPTER 7

THE POWER OF HIS SPIRIT

Now to him who is able to do immeasurably more than all we ask or
imagine, according to his power that is at work within us.
— EPHESIANS 3:20

Eagles can fly a few hundred feet above the ground with little assistance from the wind, but if they desire to soar, they must utilize wind currents and columns of warm rising air known as thermals. Once inside a strong thermal, an eagle can effortlessly circle to a height of ten thousand feet and then glide downward until it finds another rising air column upon which to float.[1] Using these rising currents of warm air and updrafts generated by valley edges or mountains, eagles soar with minimal effort; in fact, the most effort they exert when soaring is a rare, slight flip of the outer feathers. Eagles spend less than two minutes flapping their wings per hour of soaring because it takes one-twentieth of the energy to glide in flight as it does to flap their wings.[2] Soaring is a unique balance between the eagle and its environment. Although eagles must be willing to try their wings, it is the wind currents that really enable them to soar.

God is opening possibilities for you to accomplish His purposes through the potential He has put in you, as you will see in this chapter. Notice that the last stage in the Learning to Soar diagram is maturity (page 20). It takes four or five years for eagles to reach full maturity, and they go through several phases of maturity. In the latter part of the diagram you can see by the numbers on either side that maturity means the eagle or disciple has taken responsibility for himself. That does not mean, however, that he is independent. One mark of an eagle's maturity is learning to depend on the wind, and for a disciple it is learning to depend on the Spirit.

GOD'S POWER

As wind causes eagles to soar, the wind of the Spirit enables us to soar. The Hebrew language in the Old Testament and the Greek language in the New Testament use the word *wind* for spirit. Jesus used the wind as an illustration when He said that we cannot anticipate where the Spirit of God will lead us any more than we can tell where the wind will blow (see John 3:8). I don't know where the wind of God's Spirit is moving in your life, but I know that He's moving all around this world. Open your wings and let the Spirit guide you with His gusts—wherever He leads.

The Holy Spirit of God resides in every Christian, but many try to live by their own physical power. Jesus wants you to operate in the Holy Spirit, and He promised, "If you then, though you are evil, know how to give good gifts to your children, how much more will your Father in heaven give the Holy Spirit to those who ask him!" (Luke 11:13).

I once thought that effective Christian discipleship and service were the result of greater dedication and effort. But after trying to be more dedicated and working harder, I was in the depths of discouragement. At my lowest point God began to teach me about the Holy Spirit. The Holy Spirit is given to us to teach, guide, empower, and use us for God's glory. I also learned that there is a difference in *having* the Spirit and *being filled* with the Spirit. Paul said, "Do not get drunk on wine, which leads to debauchery. Instead, be filled with the Spirit" (Ephesians 5:18). Most Christians insist on upholding the negative command of that verse not to be drunk with wine, but few Christians insist on the positive command to be filled with the Spirit. If your pastor preached while he was drunk, the church leaders would immediately confront him, but if he preached without being filled with the Spirit, would anyone rebuke him? All Christians are to be filled with the Spirit.

I hope by now you've noticed this isn't your typical book about eagles. Unfortunately, the reference point for most contemporary books about eagles is people. But if the analogy of an eagle in Scripture were to begin with you, you'd probably have grown weary of the cliché motivations you've heard over and over again: be the wind beneath someone's wings; dig deep inside yourself; flap harder; soar higher; be all that you can be. Thankfully, Scripture's references to eagles don't begin with us, though they include us. The Bible's metaphors, and the Bible as a whole, begin and end with God. God doesn't stir your nest or hover over you just so you will be a better person or do nicer things. He has a plan for your life — yes — but that plan is for you to be a part of His greater plans. Next time God interacts with you, don't ask, "What's in this for me?" Rather, ask Him, "What's in this for You?" God lends us His power to work for His purposes: "For from him and through him and to him are all things" (Romans 11:36).

While I was still a freshman in college after God challenged me to be a true disciple, the Holy Spirit created in my heart an overwhelming desire to bear witness to Christ. In the months that followed, His presence overcame my natural shyness and thrust me out several times each week onto the streets and into bars to witness. However, I was not successful in leading people to Christ. I memorized Scripture, studied soul-winning books, and prayed. But something was missing.

One day I received in the mail a booklet that told of the experiences of D. L. Moody, R. A. Torrey, Billy Sunday, Billy Graham, and others whose ministries had been transformed when they experienced the filling of the Holy Spirit.

I knew that was what I needed, but I could not find anyone who could tell me how to be filled with the Spirit. Finally, a friend loaned me the book *The Holy Spirit: Who He Is and What He Does and How to Know Him in All the Fulness of His Gracious and Glorious Ministry* by R. A. Torrey. For the first time, I realized that the Holy Spirit is a person who possesses us instead of a power or an influence that we possess. Torrey showed that the Holy Spirit, who lives within us, wants to fill us for His service. By the next evening I had finished the book and was ready to follow its instructions on being filled with the Spirit. I confessed all my sins, presented myself fully to God, and asked in faith for the Holy Spirit to fill all of me.

As I confessed my sins, I realized how much the Holy Spirit loved me and had been grieved by my ignoring Him. Then I presented my body, will, emotions, intellect, and spirit to be used by God in any way. The most difficult part was accepting by faith the filling of the Holy Spirit as Torrey taught—without any outward sign or manifestation. I told God, "I will accept the fact that I am filled with the Spirit on the basis of faith in the Word, no matter what happens when I witness." There was no great emotional experience, but I had a deep awareness of the love of the Spirit.

The next day I was so aware of the Spirit's presence that I wanted to move over on the sidewalk to let Him walk beside me. That evening I witnessed to a boy on the street, and he accepted Christ as his Savior. Two nights later two teenagers accepted Christ. The following night a man professed faith in Christ.

I remarked to a friend, "I don't see how this can continue. Every night I go out to witness, someone accepts Christ." That night no one did. I had to come back and ask forgiveness and be filled afresh because I had dared to think that I had won those people to Christ myself.[3]

The scripture "Be filled with the Spirit" (Ephesians 5:18) uses the present continuous verb tense, which the International Standard Version translates, "keep on being filled with the Spirit." After I had experienced the power of the Spirit in my life, I had become presumptuous and expected the Spirit to work anytime I was ready to do anything for Him. He didn't. From that time on, I made up my mind to seek a fresh infilling of the Spirit daily. In addition, every time I have had an opportunity to serve God since then, I have specifically asked Him to refill me with the Spirit for that act of service. It's not enough to fill your car with gas the first time you drive it away from the car dealership; you need to keep on refueling it if you expect it to keep on running.

The initial filling of the Spirit is received much like salvation. We all receive the Holy Spirit by faith when we believe in Christ and are born again (see Romans 8:16-17). Some people allow the Spirit to fill all of them when they first give their lives to Christ, but most new Christians are not even told anything about being filled with God's Spirit. Here are three simple steps to be filled with the Spirit:

1. Confess all your sins to God (see 1 John 1:9).
2. Commit to do whatever God tells you to do (see Romans 12:1-2).
3. Call on God in faith to fill all of you (see Luke 11:13).

Our part is to ask and believe; God's part is to fill us with the Spirit. I remember two things R. A. Torrey wrote. He said, "Don't wait for an experiential evidence of a spiritual gift but ask in faith. Don't bring the Bible down to your experience; bring your experience up to the Bible by faith." Then He gave me a verse that convinced me to stand on the naked Word of God: "This is the confidence we have in approaching God: that if we ask anything according to his will, he hears us. And if we know that he hears us—whatever we ask—we know that we have what we asked of him" (1 John 5:14-15).

My great-granddad Avery T. Willis Sr. let the Spirit carry him from a farm in Tennessee to churches around the country. His story taught me how God can take anyone and use him. He had quit school in the seventh grade, but when he was nineteen years old, he was saved and God called him to preach. An audience of mules on the farm heard his first sermon! Afterward, he cried, "God, I told You I can't preach. Go get someone educated to preach." Suddenly, he couldn't breathe and rolled across several corn rows gasping for air. He quickly prayed, "God, if You'll let me up, I'll preach in New York City or anywhere else!"

He returned to the seventh-grade classroom at nineteen years of age only because the Holy Spirit was directing him. After graduating high school, he wrote to three colleges about admission. He prayed over their three answers without opening the letters; he asked God to lead him to open the letter from the school He wanted him to attend. The letter he opened was from Southern Baptist College in Paragould, Arkansas. It was the middle of the Great Depression and he had no money, but he went to the school to enroll anyway, arriving on campus with $2.54 in his pocket. When the dean told him that was not enough to attend, he retorted, "You tell God that. He's the One who sent me here!" The dean hesitantly offered him a work scholarship, and eventually he graduated and ministered for more than fifty years as an evangelist, church starter, and pastor. In fact, I earned my master's degree from the same seminary from which he and his son, Avery Jr., graduated. And it all began with a seventh-grade dropout who learned to soar by the power of the Spirit.

God invites you to respond to His command to be filled with the Holy Spirit. If you want to soar in life and service, you will have to do it by the power of God's Spirit.

GOD'S PURPOSES

Just as eagles must flap their wings to move into thermals in order to soar, it is important that you move into the updraft of God's purposes to join Him on mission. And just as thermals enable eagles to migrate up to 270 miles in a single day,[4] the Holy Spirit can take you further than you have ever imagined. If you choose to go in your own direction through life without seeking God's purposes, you'll waste your energy and never fly as high or as far as God could take you.

Soaring by faith is not asking God's blessings on your own flights but rather riding His purposes for you as He leads wherever He chooses. If you ask God to fulfill His purpose for you, He'll do it (see Psalm 57:2). When you place your faith in God to empower and direct you in flight, He will renew your strength like that of the eagle (see Isaiah 40:31).

All of us would like to have a soaring faith that takes us effortlessly through the shifting winds of life, but so often we muddle through like fledgling eaglets. And maybe that's good enough for you—does it really matter if eagles are regal and soar when they can get by on so much less? Similarly, some Christians are satisfied with life as it is. "Do I really need God to do amazing things through my life?" they ask. If you're tempted to settle for staying at low, safer altitudes like a juvenile eagle, you're missing out on God's ways. God made you to fly high! Ask yourself, "What am I doing in life that requires God's power?" If you strive only for pragmatic, feasible endeavors that can be accomplished without God's power, you will never soar in God's grandest purposes.

So what purpose did God have for leading the Israelites to soar out of Egypt? It included the Promised Land, but the main reason God led them there was not for physical blessings but to bring them to Himself (see Exodus 19:4). Ultimately He was fulfilling His promise to Abraham that He would set apart Abraham's descendants for His name and renown (see Genesis 17:7-8) and bless all the peoples of the earth through him. God's purposes for people revolve around Him. He gave the Israelites *His* commandments to obey *His* ways and grow in *His* righteousness (see Exodus 20:1-17). He revealed *His* presence at Mount Sinai so that the Israelites would be in awe of *His* glory and *His* holiness (see Exodus 20:18). He instructed them to build a tabernacle and temple so that all people could worship *Him* (see 1 Kings 8:43). He issued a covenant with all of *His* people to be priests that continually serve before *Him* and the nations (see 1 Peter 2:9). The purpose of God's leading us to maturity is to move us further from ourselves and closer to *Him* (see John 3:30).

After forty years of flapping and crashing, the Israelites were ready to fulfill God's purpose for bringing them out of Egypt on eagles' wings. He appointed Joshua—one of the two faithful spies who had originally explored the Promised Land—to lead them into it (see Numbers 14:30). God encouraged Joshua to be strong and courageous because He would be with him (see Joshua 1:2-9).

Reflect on how far you have come in the process from stirring to soaring. Could you be so satisfied with coming this far that you fail to step into the amazing things God has planned for you? Compare your situation with Joshua's challenge. God commanded him to lead approximately two million people to cross the flooded Jordan River into the hostile Promised Land and promised that He would go with them. God had been preparing Joshua for years for this life-shaping climax, and he knew it.

Joshua could have irresponsibly reminded God that he didn't have a track record of leading except for the time he led Israel to defeat the Amalekites forty years earlier, and even that required Moses' help (see Exodus 17:9-14). He could have reminded God that it had been easier for Moses to lead the Israelites across the Red Sea. As Henry and Richard Blackaby have noted,

> Moses could at least stand still and watch the waters of the Red Sea divide before him. But Joshua was commanded to march directly into the river; the only indication it would miraculously subside was God's promise that it would.
>
> Only when the priests' toes entered the swirling waters did the river's flow cease. God could have parted the river the night

before . . . the Israelites arrived. But He chose to stretch their faith.[5]

The normally quiet, meandering Jordan had become a raging river a mile wide at flood tide. What if the Israelites again refused to risk their lives, as their forefathers had done forty years earlier when God told them to enter the Promised Land the first time? What if the river did not stop flowing?

All Joshua had was God's Spirit and His Word. When all you have is God, you realize that's all you need! Joshua boldly commanded the priests to stand in the middle of the river. The miracle did not happen until the exact moment the priests' feet touched the river's edge (see Joshua 3:15-16). Then the priests marched to the middle of the Jordan and stood firm on dry ground until all Israel had marched across the Jordan River.

Are you standing at the edge of your personal Jordan wondering if you can trust God to open up an impossible situation and take you through it? He has brought you to this place to show His amazing power and presence. Put your feet in the water and let God fulfill His purpose for you!

GOD-GIVEN POTENTIAL

God made us to soar as eagles and fulfill the potential He gave us when He made us. When a manufacturer makes a product, he builds into it the potential to fulfill its purpose. I once rented a car in Germany and was upgraded to a Mercedes. I started driving on the autobahn at about sixty-five miles per hour. Because there was no speed limit, cars were passing me like I was standing still. Irritated drivers rode my bumper and honked their horns until I changed lanes. I finally sped up to about 120 miles per hour as our children cheered me on while my wife urged me to slow down! The experience scared me—not just because I was driving so fast but because I still wasn't going fast enough! I couldn't bring myself to go the full 180 miles per hour, but the car had the potential to go that fast. What would your life look like today if you fulfilled the entire potential God built into you instead of falling short because of your own perceived limitations? Put the pedal to the metal!

LIVING UP TO YOUR POTENTIAL

Your Manufacturer has placed in you a potential that can be achieved only by operating in the Spirit by faith. Unfortunately, we don't come with a sticker telling us our potential, as cars do, so we must "test-drive" our potential to fully discover it. A machine's potential is squandered if it is used for less than it was intended. You would waste a chain saw's potential if you used it to cut weeds. If you don't live up to God's purposes, you squander your potential.

God built us to excel. He gives us our potential through physical capabilities and spiritual gifts. "All these are the work of one and the same Spirit, and he gives them to each one, just as he determines" (1 Corinthians 12:11). Although we can't choose our spiritual gifts, our faith determines their effectiveness (see Romans 12:6). Because capabilities and limitations vary with each person, God does not want you to compare yourself with others (see 2 Corinthians 10:12). Instead, you should compare yourself with the person God intended you to be. Success is best measured by what you do yourself in comparison to what God could do in you.

If you already have the potential, why do you need to pray? Receiving potential from God and trying to do things without ever talking to Him is like trying to clean the carpet with an unplugged vacuum cleaner — you will put out effort, but you won't make much of a difference.

I used to recycle only two generic prayers: "bless everyone" and "thank You for everything." A small prayer notebook greatly increased and deepened my prayer requests. In it, I have divided up urgent prayer requests (for the friend who has surgery next Tuesday), different prayers for each weekday (for myself, my family, and ministries), and prayer requests for each day of the month (friends, national leaders, social issues). You can buy a pocket-size composite notebook and form it however you want. Take it with you on the go and see how intentional and meaningful your prayers can be.

When I visited the Middle East, a Muslim friend of mine had learned about Jesus and wanted to follow Him if only he could see Him in a dream. I told him I would pray that God would answer his request. For two weeks, I prayed that the Holy Spirit would reveal Himself in a dream to my friend, yet he experienced nothing — so I recruited more people to pray. Then he dreamed Jesus was on a glowing path to God; he believed in Him, and Jesus came to reside inside him. This man became a true follower of Jesus by God's power as a result of prayer.

PRAYING YOUR POTENTIAL

You may think you have already reached your potential. When Bruce Wilkinson gave me an early copy of *The Prayer of Jabez* at Billy Graham's Amsterdam 2000 conference, I questioned the section on asking God to "enlarge my territory." I wondered how God could enlarge my territory any more when my responsibility with the International Mission Board was to lead 5,600 missionaries in 183 countries around the world. Besides, I was only a few years from retirement! I dismissed that part of the book until I invited Bruce to teach his course on *The Vision of the Leader* to our world leaders. Bruce explained that Jabez was asking for more influence, more responsibility, and more opportunity to make a mark for God. God again challenged me to pray that I could make a greater impact for Him.

I had two life-altering experiences at Billy Graham's Amsterdam 2000 conference. The organizers asked five hundred global missions leaders how we could get the gospel to all the unengaged, unreached people groups of the world. We sat at tables strategizing, and at Table 71, several of us who were leaders of major missions organizations committed ourselves and our organizations to work together to "just do it." Our goal was zero unreached people groups. That was not a new goal for me but a new level of cooperation among missions agencies. We have met three times a year ever since, and God has spawned several movements including OneStory, Finishing the Task, and Call2All—with real progress being made.[6]

A second life-changing experience happened as we were packing up our things to leave the conference. Marcus Vegh, a friend who had a deep concern for unreached people groups and oral learners, came over to the table and asked me, "How do you disciple oral learners? Seventy percent of the unreached people are functionally illiterate."

I replied, "I don't know. People have asked me that question for twenty years, and I just reply, 'I'm not working with illiterate people. If you are, figure it out.'"

Marcus pointed his finger in my face and said, "That's your job. You know something about discipleship; find out how to do it!" I heard his voice as the voice of God because we had just learned that 70 percent of the unreached people of the world are functionally illiterate. I have dedicated the rest of my life to help the body of Christ disciple all oral learners. The orality movement has spread all over the world and is now affecting the United States as well—where we are teaching churches and organizations to reach the 50 percent of Americans who are oral learners, plus the millennials who can read but don't like to. In fact, the Discussion Guide for Small Groups on page 143 uses these Bible Storying principles that Jesus used to transform lives.

I can assure you that God has certainly enlarged my territory. God did what I thought was impossible. He expanded my influence and service beyond anything I had ever experienced.

Are you approaching the fullness of your potential in spiritual growth and influence, or have you stopped short of what God intended? Ask God to expand your borders of influence and fulfill the potential He has for you. The following prayer points can guide you as you realize God's potential in you:

- Before you pray about your current circumstance, seek God's will and ask Him to clean your heart of any impure motivations (see Psalm 66:18; 1 John 5:14).
- While you pray, be real with God. He knows who you are, so don't guard your emotions or be afraid to say certain things.
- When God answers a prayer in the way you asked Him, thank Him. Also, write it down so that you will trust Him more in future prayers.
- When God seems not to be responding to you, believe that He acts in accordance with His will. Continue to pray and ask God to conform you and your prayer to His will.
- When God answers your prayer differently than you would have liked, accept it and place your faith in His wisdom.
- Whenever you pray, regardless of how God may respond, praise and thank Him for listening to and loving you.

PUTTING YOUR POTENTIAL INTO PRACTICE

Procrastination, peer pressure, sin, and fear are obstacles that preclude faith from operating—and also immobilize your potential. Procrastination tells God, "I'll do it someday." Be aware that God does allow you to go your own way and waste your chances to do something great. Regarding peer pressure, if God has given you a vision, don't let others take it away from you. Your true capacity is not limited, reduced, or altered by your previous failures or the opinions of others. Sin always limits what God will do through you. Though some consequences of sin are irreversible, God's grace allows you to fulfill His purposes for the rest of your life if you repent and obey Him.

Karen Bennett didn't yield to fear and thus tapped into her God-given potential. After she graduated from college, Karen moved to inner-city Atlanta and lived in an abandoned nightclub without heat or air-conditioning, a shower, or even a toilet. She risked her life to minister to the youth in that area. She was beaten up, the windows of her vehicle were shot out, and ten of the first teenagers she met were murdered. She pressed on and established a youth church and a school. The church has experienced seventy break-ins, but her ministry now affects three thousand lives each week because she didn't shy away from what God led her to do. She said, "If you decide that what God is asking you to do with your life is just too much for you and is just a little too inconvenient, then you will never see the miracles He has for you."[7]

God works mightily through you when you put your faith to work first. Even though God's power accomplishes the work, you still must take the first step of faith. God was strong enough to part the Red Sea for the Israelites without human assistance—but before He did anything, He told Moses to lift his staff over the water (see Exodus 14:16). Later, God miraculously parted the waters of the Jordan River for the Israelites to cross—but not until the soles of the priests' feet touched the water (see Joshua 3:15-16). God made the walls of Jericho fall as the Israelites entered the Promised Land—but not until, by faith, they marched around the walls for seven days and then seven times on the last day (see Joshua 6:3,15,20).

God put the potential in you; He expects you to work it out. Faith requires action as evidenced by those in the Hall of Faith in Hebrews

11. Every illustration of faith shows the person actively responding to God. Abel offered a sacrifice. Enoch walked with God. Noah built an ark. Abraham moved to a distant country. Isaac laid himself on the sacrificial altar. Jacob blessed his children, acting on faith in God's promise to bless his descendants. Joseph forgave his brothers and spoke to his children about the Exodus almost four hundred years before it happened. Moses refused to stay in Pharaoh's house and through his faith and actions delivered the Israelites from Egypt. Even Rahab the prostitute hid the spies. Has God made His point yet? Faith works as you work.

As writer Curtis Grant said, "People who want milk shouldn't sit on a stool in the middle of a field in hopes that a cow will back up to them."[8] God admonishes you to "continue to work out your salvation with fear and trembling, for it is God who works in you to will and to act according to his good purpose" (Philippians 2:12-13). If you do not put your God-given abilities to work, they will deteriorate with time, just as muscles that are not used slowly atrophy. Faith without works is dead; so are works without the Spirit. Follow God's Word in Zechariah 4:6: "'Not by might nor by power, but by my Spirit,' says the LORD Almighty."

Let the Spirit be the wind, open your wings, and soar!

LET'S GET PERSONAL HERE

1. Can you recall an example from your past in which you know you fell short of what God wanted to do in or through you?
2. In what new ways can you allow God's Spirit and power to flow through you?
3. When was the last time you asked His Spirit to fill all of you? What does it mean to live daily in the Spirit?
4. How close are you to experiencing the full potential God has placed in you?
5. What false limitations have you believed about yourself and about God?
6. What do you think God is leading you to do next?

CHAPTER 8

SOAR ABOVE THE STORMS

They will soar on wings like eagles;
they will run and not grow weary,
they will walk and not be faint.
— ISAIAH 40:31

Maturity is more than learning to fly and riding the thermals. Eagles also have to learn to forage for themselves, migrate in winter, find a mate, reproduce, and go through the parenting process with their offspring.

After a parent eagle teaches its young eagle how to soar, it shows it how to fly above the storms. When bad weather comes, an eagle sets the pitch of its wings to catch the wind so it will be effortlessly buoyed up above the storm.[1] Eagles can survive storms, but they must learn to soar above them so they can migrate and make it through their first winter.

As soaring is more than just a convenient cruise available to eagles, soaring in faith is more than just a luxurious option for Christians. It is a necessity. When arctic storms challenge you like never before, will you be ready to pitch your wings in faith and rise above them, or will you try to hibernate? Eagles don't hibernate!

I faced an intense, figurative storm once in South Africa. Before you read about this experience, however, this would be a good time to stop and review the essential points of getting and acting on a word from God (chapter 6, pages 98–104). Then see how I used them to overcome my obstacles.

I was teaching a *MasterLife* discipleship workshop to leaders from nine countries in southern Africa. My plan was to do the same for leaders from eight east African countries the next week in Kenya. In the middle of the first week, the Kenyan government banned anyone with a passport containing a South Africa stamp from entering Kenya.

Meanwhile the leaders in South Africa and east Africa prayed diligently for me. I sought God's guidance in my regular Bible reading and read Psalm 118 the day before I was to leave. The following verses leaped off the page at me, and I felt the Holy Spirit applying them to my desperate situation:

> In my anguish I cried to the LORD,
>   and he answered by setting me free.
> The LORD is with me; I will not be afraid.
>   What can man do to me? . . .
> All the nations surrounded me,
>   but in the name of the LORD I cut them off. . . .
> I was pushed back and about to fall,
>   but the LORD helped me.
> The LORD is my strength and my song;
>   he has become my salvation.
> Shouts of joy and victory
>   resound in the tents of the righteous:
> "The LORD's right hand has done mighty things!" (Psalm
>   118:5-6,10,13-15)

I believed that this was a word from God telling me that I would make it to Kenya. I discussed it with my friend Tom Elliff, who had helped me apply a word from God to other difficult situations. He responded, "I am praying that the people in Nairobi will greet you with shouts of joy and praise to the Lord because He has gotten you in." Then I shared the word from God with those attending the workshop, and they joined me in affirmation and prayer.

In an attempt to get around the ban, my wife and I went to Zimbabwe first. We arrived at four o'clock on a Friday afternoon, and we had to get new passports, new visas, and new tickets by five o'clock. Talk about an impossible situation! It would take at least three weeks to do that in the United States—but by God's grace and the help of a short-term missionary, we got them before the offices closed. I give all glory to God because only God could have made that happen!

The next morning, an immigration official said we could not board the plane because our passports weren't twenty-four hours old. He asked, "Where are your other passports?" Because they contained a South Africa visa, I had put them in our luggage that had already been checked. He said, "You can't go because they won't let you disembark in Kenya. They will make you stay on the plane to Europe."

After arguing with him for several minutes I asked, "Is this your problem, or is it my problem?"

"It's your problem because they won't let you off the plane."

I replied, "If it is my problem, let me handle it. If they won't let me off, it is not your problem."

"Okay," he said with his hands uplifted and a resigned look on his face. "It's your problem."

If I had not believed the word from God, I would not have started on the trip; I would not have gone to all the trouble to get the new documents; and certainly I would not have negotiated so hard with the official. It *does* matter whether you believe when you face difficulties! When we got to Kenya, the three people in front of us were not allowed to disembark, but the official quickly stamped our passports and welcomed us to Kenya. The parking lot resounded with shouts of joy and victory by the workshop participants who escorted us out. The Lord's mighty hand still does great things through us when we soar with Him above the storms through faith in His Word!

The eagle uses storms for its benefit, and a healthy Christian does the same. Your greatest opportunity to soar in faith is when the storms of life come—times of uncertainty, fear, and adversity. Some of these storms can't be avoided, but as you place your faith in the Lord in the midst of them, the Holy Spirit will strengthen you and lift you above the storms.

Don't stay grounded—pitch your wings of faith and catch the wind of the Spirit.

GOD'S PERSPECTIVE

Do you try to look at the storms in life as God sees them? Changing your perspective to God's perspective does not prevent storms, but it encourages you to overcome them. For example, people used to believe that no one could run a mile in less than four minutes. However, that view changed when Roger Bannister broke that barrier in 1954. Since then, more than one thousand sprinters have run a sub–four-minute mile, and the fastest time for the mile is presently 3:43.[2] I don't know how your perspective compares with God's perspective for your life, but God wants you to see things from His eternal viewpoint.

An eagle's eyesight is astounding. If eagles were literate, they could read this book from across a football field![3] Unlike humans, who look straight ahead and focus directly on an object, eagles have the ability to look both forward and sideways simultaneously as they dive.[4] Because of their great vision, eagles can see a moving rabbit one mile away; you couldn't see one that far away if you used binoculars.[5] Occasionally, an eagle can spot a fish from two miles away,[6] and if an eagle flies high enough, it can see another eagle soaring nearly fifty miles away.[7]

Sight is much different from vision, and our position determines our perspective. Even fully grown eagles are unable to see over the outer edge of their nest if they stand in the middle of it.[8] Just as an eagle's capability of seeing greater distances increases with the height of its flight, so God helps you experience the full potential of your faith as you increasingly practice it. When you soar where God leads you, He gives you a brand-new perspective on life.

On a vacation, Shirley and I visited Mount Rushmore, where the heads of four American presidents are carved out of a 5,725-foot mountain. Each head is sixty feet high.[9] Although this historical landmark is impressive, it was not what challenged my perspective. Crazy Horse did.

Crazy Horse is a monument being carved out of a nearby mountain in the Black Hills of South Dakota. After the Rushmore monument was sculped out of the mountain, Lakota Chief Henry Standing Bear wrote to sculptor Korczak Ziolkowski in 1939, telling him that he and other Native American chiefs wanted the white man to know that the "red man" also had great heroes.[10]

Korczak began working on the project in 1948. He married his wife, Ruth, in 1950, and they had ten children—seven of whom are still working on the sculpture. When Korczak died in 1982, he had only blocked out the mountain, written specifications for the monument, and carefully made models to scale.[11]

The face of the Crazy Horse monument was completed and unveiled in 1998—fifty years after Korczak started! Crazy Horse's completed head is eighty-seven feet high; all four of the Mount Rushmore busts could fit inside it. When finished, the Crazy Horse monument will stand 641 feet long and 563 feet high.[12] That makes it the tallest memorial in the world—taller than the Statue of Liberty, the Washington Monument, and the Pyramids.

The Holy Spirit enables us to rise above our natural selves. He can bring us out above our manmade storms: racism, war, injustice, divisions, revenge, sexual abuse, and political corruption. The disciple Peter is a great example of someone God helped to soar above racism. Peter was a full-blooded Jew. Cornelius was a non-Jewish man who desperately wanted to know God. God sent liaisons from Cornelius to invite Peter into his home so that Cornelius could receive the message of the gospel. At the same time the messengers were traveling, God told Peter that nothing He had made was impure. Peter went with them to see Cornelius, and as he entered the house, he admitted, "It is against our law for a Jew to associate with a Gentile or visit him. But God has shown me that I should not call any man impure or unclean" (Acts 10:28).

It pains me, as a Caucasian, that my ancestors have been some of the worst culprits of racism. Even in the past few years, I have heard Caucasians make derogatory racist remarks without even recognizing them. Praise God that we can fly over walls of racism by His power; we must pray that He continues to overpower the racism that still remains in our cultures.

No one can predict when the sculpture will be completed. It could even be a hundred years after Korczak started his work. That is what blew my mind! He committed himself to a vision that could not be completed in his lifetime. I sensed God asking me if I was working on such a big vision that it could not be completed in my lifetime. How about you? How big is your vision?

RUN AND FLY

God points us again to the eagle in Isaiah 40:30-31 to show that discipleship not only is flying but also includes running toward God's purpose, walking our talk, and even waiting in preparation:

> Though youths grow weary and tired,
> And vigorous young men stumble badly,
> Yet those who wait for the LORD
> Will gain new strength;
> They will mount up with wings like eagles,
> They will run and not get tired,
> They will walk and not become weary. (NASB)

It may seem unusual to describe faith with the word *waiting* since we traditionally think of faith as *following*. However, eagles realize the importance of waiting before soaring. If no strong winds are available, an eagle will stay perched in a tree and wait until they come.[13] If eagles spread their wings to fly without waiting for wind support, they wear themselves out. Any attempt of ours to work for God will be ineffective without first waiting for the Spirit's direction and empowerment.

Although I've heard or read these verses from Isaiah 40 so many times in sermons, at youth rallies, in graduation cards, and in my personal Bible reading, I still love them. I'm an energetic person, yet I get so exhausted at times — "though youths grow weary and tired" — especially when it comes to needing sleep. Why did God create sleep? I believe He made it to remind us of our need to depend on Him and of His superiority to us. Even the world's worst workaholics still need to sleep. However, waiting for the Lord does not come as automatically as sleep.

Waiting for God does not mean you live your own way until God comes and interrupts your schedule. It means that you actively anticipate God's giving you an opportunity to be involved with Him. Have you ever had a server really wait on you in a restaurant? One time, my wife and I had the privilege of eating at a fancy restaurant at which a server expectantly stood nearby to scrape crumbs off our table. We should wait on God in the same way, eager to do something for Him as menial as scraping up crumbs (see Psalm 84:10). A waiting faith is a surrendered availability, a dependency upon God's presence. Don't try to follow God without first waiting for His direction. He "acts on behalf of those who wait for him" (Isaiah 64:4).

REPRODUCE

When eagles reproduce, you know they have reached maturity. After eagles reach full adulthood, they mate for life. When the winter storms rage, they make their way to the moderate southern areas where they were raised, build a nest, and begin the process all over again. Sometimes it is a storm to go through the mentoring process with your offspring. What the eagle does by instinct, we need to do on purpose — reproduce! No doubt you can look back and see how people have invested in you. Now it is time for you to invest in others coming after you.

MENTORING OTHERS

Most leaders in the Bible had a mentor or mentors who helped them at a strategic time in their lives, often over a long period of time. Moses was mentored by his father-in-law, Jethro, and Moses passed on the model by discipling Joshua.

We first meet Joshua soon after Israel left Egypt. Moses told Joshua to lead Israel to fight the Amalekites who had attacked them, and then he stood on the mountain overlooking the battle and raised his hands while Joshua and Israel's troops fought. As long as Moses held his hands up to the Lord, Joshua's troops prevailed—but when Moses' arms grew tired, the Israelites began to lose. That experience symbolizes the process Moses used to mentor Joshua and prepare him to lead Israel into the Promised Land.

When Israel fearfully refused to enter the Promised Land, Moses took Joshua as his constant companion. We don't hear much about Joshua for the next forty years because he stayed in the Tent of Meeting, where he and Moses met the Lord. After Moses died, God called Joshua to help Israel ride on the high places of the earth and take the Promised Land (see Deuteronomy 32:13; Joshua 1:1-5).

Other biblical examples of the mentoring process include Elijah and Elisha, Eli and Samuel, Barnabas and Paul, and Paul and Timothy. Mentors have a gift of seeing potential in others. They help them understand themselves, discover their gifts, and realize how they affect other people. Mentors give them a personal model to follow and disciple them to follow Christ and become like Him. They improve their skills, recommend them to others, open doors for them, defend them, and encourage them.

I have had many mentors in my life, but a man in The Navigators showed me what a disciple-maker and mentor is. Soon after I started a church in Fort Worth, Texas, while in seminary, I began attending Saturday night Bible studies in Dallas at the home of this Navigator. I continually asked the leaders about their secret of discipling people, but for weeks they just encouraged me to attend the general meetings. Finally, when Skip Grey, the leader, was convinced that I was serious, he started driving to Fort Worth every week to spend an hour with me. He always brought someone with him to disciple on the way but met me alone. What amazed me was that this busy leader would drive two hours to spend an hour alone with me. I thought, *I would drive to Dallas to speak to a crowd, but I doubt I would do it for one person.* Following his example, I have committed my life to making disciples who make disciples.

A few months later, I heard a tape of *Born to Reproduce* by Dawson

Trotman, the founder of The Navigators, that shaped my life.[14] He began to disciple a sailor friend, Les Spencer, in 1934. One night as they were sitting in the car reviewing memory verses, a policeman asked what they were doing. Dawson showed him Bible verse after Bible verse and led the policeman to faith in Christ. On their way back home, Les said, "Boy, I'd give my right arm to know how to use the Word like that."

"No, you wouldn't," replied Daws.

"I said that I would give my right arm to do that," rejoined Les emphatically.

Daws said that it would take at least that much discipline, but he was willing to show Les how if he would commit himself to learn to do it. Les kept his word, became a disciple, and then began looking for a man on his ship to disciple. When he found him, he said to Daws, "Do with him what you did with me."

Daws refused and said, "If you can't do with him what I have done with you, I have failed."

That was the beginning of the ministry of The Navigators. By the time Les's ship was sunk at Pearl Harbor, 125 men had been led to Christ. Daws summed it up:

Men off that first battleship are in four continents of the world as missionaries today. The work spread from ship to ship to ship, so that when the Japanese struck at Pearl Harbor, there was a testimony being given on fifty ships of the U.S. fleet. When the war closed, there was work by one or more producers (I am not talking about mere Christians), on more than a thousand of the U.S. Fleet ships and at many army camps and air bases.[15]

His story inspired me to give my life to reproducing disciples who would reproduce disciples.

As I was proposing this book at Glen Eyrie, the headquarters for The Navigators in Colorado Springs, Colorado, I went to Dawson's graveside high in the mountains where the eagles nested. When I read his birth date on his tombstone, I realized that Daws was born the same month as my father. I wrote in my journal, "I was shaped and directed by these two men more than any others. Dad shaped and molded my character along with my mom, but Daws led me to dedicate my life to making disciples of all nations."

At Daws' graveside, God renewed His vision for my life—to help His church return to Jesus' method of making disciples using oral means, by Bible Storying.[16] I reread Daws' life verse that I had adopted as my own many years before: "And they that shall be of thee shall build the old waste places: thou shalt raise up the foundations of many generations; and thou shalt be called, The repairer of the breach, The restorer of the paths to dwell in" (Isaiah 58:12, KJV). Then I wrote, "I like the KJV version of 'repairer of the breach' because I believe there is a breach in Your church—a gap in discipleship—and I want to be a 'restorer of the paths to dwell in' and have my spiritual descendants 'raise up the foundations of many generations.'"

Please don't miss the point of this book. Life is not about how you can climb the ladder of success. God doesn't exist so that you can fly or so that you can stand on His shoulders. Jesus is our ultimate example, and He humbled Himself on this earth with the goal of glorifying God the Father (see Philippians 2:11). He showed us that we should live more for others than for ourselves, as Paul prescribed a few verses earlier: "Do nothing out of selfish ambition or vain conceit, but in humility consider others better than yourselves. Each of you should look not only to your own interests, but also to the interests of others" (verses 3-4). When we recognize the humility that Jesus Christ showed us by coming to this earth, we must no longer seek status.

Thus, don't seek out a mentor just so that you can improve yourself and gain a better reputation. If you only receive spiritual instruction but do not give, you are like the Dead Sea, which is 8.6 times saltier than the ocean.[17] The Dead Sea only *receives* nutrients — it has no outlet river to *pass on* life. Any fish that swims into the Dead Sea dies immediately. Many adults erroneously think of our walk with God as a container that we need to fill up with God rather than as a conduit with which we freely give and receive God.

Pass on God's ways to your learner (Timothy) one-on-one or to several learners at a time in a group setting. Not sure what to share with your Timothy? I like to share my life story, practical tools I have discovered for spiritual disciplines like prayer and reading the Bible, and then specific topics that my Timothy wants to learn.

Have you reached the place of maturity where you are a reproducer of disciples who reproduce? Are you setting the pace? Do you need to be finding a Les Spencer to disciple? Do you need to disciple your own children or grandchildren? God has taught you to soar through the storms of life so you can fulfill His purposes for you.

If you feel you are not yet mature enough to make disciples, start with finding someone to disciple and mentor you. Soon you will realize that every Spirit-filled believer has something to offer a fellow brother or sister in the faith. If you are mature, reproduce!

GOD LIFTS US OVER THE STORMS

God is diligent in seeing His purposes accomplished among all people all the time. He shows us how to reach a height that influences the kingdom beyond our own lives.

God lifts His people over storms when they want to give up. Look at the rest of the martyrs of the Hall of Faith in Hebrews 11:

> Others were tortured and refused to be released, so that they might gain a better resurrection. Some faced jeers and flogging, while still others were chained and put in prison. They were stoned; they were sawed in two; they were put to death by the sword. They went about in sheepskins and goatskins, destitute, persecuted and mistreated—the world was not worthy of them. They wandered in deserts and mountains, and in caves and holes in the ground. These were all commended for their faith, yet none of them received what had been promised. God had planned something better for us so that only together with us would they be made perfect.
>
> Therefore, since we are surrounded by such a great cloud of witnesses, let us throw off everything that hinders and the sin that so easily entangles, and let us run with perseverance the race marked out for us. Let us fix our eyes on Jesus, the author and perfecter of our faith, who for the joy set before him endured the cross, scorning its shame, and sat down at the right hand of the throne of God. (Hebrews 11:35–12:2)

I believe that we live at the hinge of history. God is giving you the opportunity to soar over the storms in your life as the people in Hebrews 11 and Jesus our Lord did. Their sacrifice is made perfect or complete through what we do in our day. You are running a relay race that spans many millennia. The baton is extended to you—grab it and fly!

Here is a modern example of this perseverance and reproduction through a friend of mine, whom I'll call Abdul. As a thirteen-year-old boy in a country that was 85 percent Muslim, he was condemned, rejected, beaten, and ultimately banished from his Islamic school by his teachers because he kept asking questions about the Koran. They told him that he was not to question the Koran but to simply accept it. The *imam* branded him a sinner and issued a decree that no one should speak to him, not even his own family. For five years he lived in a little house behind his parents' home; his only contact with people was when his mother brought his meals and left them outside his door. He tried to commit suicide three times.

One hot day in May, Abdul was walking along the road when he heard a man in a rickshaw ask in his language, "Hey, brother, would you like to ride with me?"

Abdul thought, *Oh, there is no one else here, so this man must be talking to me.*

He told me, "I answered yes because nobody would talk with me, yet this man called me brother. I got in the rickshaw, and he was so nice and just so good. I was a condemned man. Nobody wanted to talk with me. I thought, *Why is he so good to me?* I wondered if he was a man or angel, so I touched his hand again and again to be sure he was a man."

The man in the rickshaw was Tom Thurman, a longtime missionary to Hindus. He took Abdul home with him for refreshments, and by the end of the day Tom and Abdul had struck up a friendship. Later, Tom gave Abdul a Bible. He read through the entire New Testament and then began to read it again. When he got to the gospel of John he read,

For God did not send his Son into the world to condemn the world, but to save the world through him. Whoever believes in him is not condemned, but whoever does not believe stands condemned already because he has not believed in the name of God's one and only Son. (3:17-18)

He accepted Christ as his Savior on the spot.

After Abdul became a Christian, he told his family. They were very upset with him, and his father and uncles beat him. Before daybreak the next morning his mother gave him some money and told him, "Son, you must run because they are going to kill you." Abdul fled to the capital of the country, found a church, and was baptized. After he finished college, Abdul heard God calling him back to the village of his youth. His banishment from home still firmly in place, Abdul stayed with a childhood friend.

Abdul told me the rest of his story:

I had my Koran and my Bible with me, and every night I shared with my friend. Within three months he accepted Christ and was ready for baptism. Then his parents found out and were very upset with me. That afternoon they forcefully took me to the soccer field, where they tied my hands behind me. They asked me about Jesus. Somebody kicked me with his boot. Somebody else hit me. Everyone spit on me until my whole body was covered by spit. I remembered when Jesus was crucified and prayed, "Father, forgive them. They do not know what they are doing. Please God, help them, save them, and forgive them."

They left Abdul for dead, but his new convert came and released him from his bonds. He then begged Abdul to baptize him, despite the torture he had just witnessed. When Abdul told him he didn't know what he was asking, his friend replied, "If you don't baptize me, you are a hypocrite." So the next morning Abdul baptized him. As they left the river, Abdul said, "Thank You, God. Yesterday afternoon I was beaten up and was the only Christian in this village. But today we are two. Tomorrow we can be two hundred. Day after tomorrow we can be two thousand, God, if You want it. Yes." Reflecting on the situation, Abdul said, "I think God listened. He listened to my prayer that day."

Then he said, "Today in that village we have 1,600 believers, all of whom had spit on me. But today all of them are believers." Abdul's mother was dead by this time, but he was able to lead his father to Christ and baptize him. Abdul's first convert began the first church in another village and became the trainer for other church planters. They began to go to the mosques and villages and ask questions to the imams about the Koran. These questions caused people to seek them out for answers, which they were able to give them from the Bible.

When I met Abdul eight years later, we had verified by on-the-ground research that the movement had grown to almost four thousand churches with ninety-three thousand baptized believers. The week before I met Abdul, his first convert, Belial, had been martyred. This man had discipled the leaders of the house churches, taking nine to twelve to live with him for three months at a time. Abdul told me, "I don't know what I am going to do since he was the one who discipled my key leaders." At his invitation, two years later I went to his country to teach his key leaders how to use Bible stories to help people experience God and make disciples. He told me that although nine of the leaders had been martyred, they had grown to 9,700 house churches with more than 450,000 baptized believers in less than ten years.

Tom Thurman summed up the story: "It all started with that rickshaw ride back a long time before that. And I was reminded of that phrase in the hymn 'Lead On, O King Eternal': 'With deeds of love and mercy the heavenly kingdom comes.'"

God can do so much more than we think when we are available to soar on the wind of the Spirit. Tom simply befriended Abdul, gave him a Bible, and taught him the basics of the Christian life, but God took this cast-out boy and started a church-planting movement that is reaching people across his country and spilling over into adjoining countries.

Abdul experienced God's stirring, hovering, challenging, and empowering. Do you have a vision so grand that it cannot be fulfilled in your lifetime? God determines your fruitfulness, and your life may bear fruit for eons to come if you are faithful. Come catch the rising wind of God's Spirit and soar above the storms!

LET'S GET PERSONAL HERE

1. If you were an eagle, where would you be in the Learning to Soar diagram (see page 20)?

2. When storms challenge you, do you pitch your wings in faith and rise above them instead of trying to hibernate? What do you think this looks like in your circumstances?

3. Do you have a Timothy—a person you are discipling? Write the names of people you can disciple. Be sure to add them to your prayer list. Consider leading them through the Learning to Soar Discussion Guide for Small Groups (see page 143).

4. Have you ever had a vision so grand that it cannot be fulfilled in your lifetime? If not, ask God to show you ways to leave a legacy.

5. Pray right now to see your life from God's perspective. What do you see? Does it surprise you?

AN EVER-
DEVELOPING STORY

He who began a good work in you will carry it on to completion until
the day of Christ Jesus.
— PHILIPPIANS 1:6

Israel did "ride on the high places" of the Promised Land by faith and received what God had guaranteed Abraham several centuries earlier, but it was a long process from stirring to soaring (Deuteronomy 32:13, NASB). And God would continually repeat the process with His people. God wanted the Israelites to remember that He stirred their nest out of Egypt and He would stir their nests again with famines, plagues, and warfare if they forsook Him (see Deuteronomy 32:24-25).

Moses' song (in Deuteronomy 32) was a wake-up call to all the Israelites who believed they had already experienced God's stirring and hovering and had finished spreading their wings and soaring. Israel was never supposed to set the cruise-control button while soaring; God was not finished with them. In the centuries after Israel entered the Promised Land, God stirred their nest multiple times for their own good and His glory. Occasionally the people of Israel responded well to God's stirring; at other times they ignored Him. But God repeatedly hovered over them, inviting them to do His will.

When the people did spread their wings to follow God, sometimes it was a short flight. At times, they crashed and burned. At other times, they returned to God and soared on His wings, becoming exactly who He had created and nurtured them to be. The stirring-to-soaring process that God had for them — and for you today — is a never-ending cycle, an ever-developing story. Therefore, just because someone is soaring right now doesn't make him or her exempt from God's stirrings in the future. As Paul warned, "If you think you are standing firm, be careful that you don't fall!" (1 Corinthians 10:12). He also said, "Forgetting what is behind and straining toward what is ahead, I press on toward the goal to win the prize for which God has called me heavenward in Christ Jesus" (Philippians 3:13-14).

Remember my friend Brandon from chapter 1 — the one God stirred using Hurricane Katrina? By God's grace, Brandon left his nest when Hurricane Katrina swept through his home, but as Brandon put it, "God's stirring wasn't complete." In less than a month after he lost virtually everything, Hurricane Rita destroyed much of the area around Lake Charles, Brandon's new home. Though he was able to escape this time with his possessions, he lost his newly acquired job; however, since Brandon had become airborne with God's first stirring, he truly soared when God stirred him again.

Brandon reflected, "Just when I thought I had responded to God's stirring obediently and that I could begin to relax in my life surroundings, my nest was shaken again. It would be easy for me to resist and fight against God's apparent stirring in my life. Nonetheless, I am able to look back and see how God's stirring has caused my faith to grow. God truly has a plan for me to continue to become more conformed to the image of Christ through this time, even though I do not fully understand all that has happened to me and to others." Brandon's school temporarily shut down, which postponed his course work. He transferred to a seminary in Texas, and while there, he met the woman who is now his wife. He recently graduated with his master's degree and is using it to serve people who have not heard of the love of God.

If only we all could have such a godly perspective when God stirs our nests!

Where are you in the stirring-to-soaring process? What is your potential in life? Only God knows, and the only way you can find out is by stepping out in faith and giving yourself to Him and to His purposes for your life.

As you have examined your life from the nest to the sky, how far has God brought you? At the beginning of this book, we talked about God stirring your nest. If you remain complacent with incomplete growth, He wants to shake up your life and focus your attention back on Him. If you positively respond to God's stirring, He shows His power and love as He hovers over you, bringing you to the realization that He is big enough to overcome your confusion, adversities, and storms.

Have you experienced the thrill of spreading your wings and flying outside the nest? You have likely experienced many transitions and trials as God has taught you His ways, developed your character, and increased your faith. You may have also been challenged to soar above storms in your life. God has shown you His purpose and wants to lift you above yourself into His marvelous plans. How far have you come? Regardless of where you are in the process, your next step is a risk—but one worth taking. Do you want to soar?

After I spoke on eagles at a spiritual-awakening conference at East Texas Baptist University, a freshman who identified herself as Marcia Tapp[1] gave me this poem that she had written as I spoke:

It's so warm in this sheltered place
So safe here from harm
I could stay here forever
Nestled in Your arms.

But now my world is changing
You're doing something new
You're asking me to place
My total trust in You.

I'm scared as I take my place
Upon Your wings, spread for flight,
As I feel You flying higher
Circling with all my might.

Slowly I dare to open my eyes
Then see more than I've ever seen.
You are taking me up to a place
Beyond my highest dreams.

How wonderful up in the heights
With my Father far above the world.
Then He whispers, "Trust me more
For I have a greater plan."

Suddenly He thrusts me into the air
I find myself falling through the sky
Fluttering helplessly, alone and scared . . .
I spread my wings—now I can fly!

As you give God everything you have, He will provide everything you need. Catch the wind of His Spirit and soar.

LET'S GET PERSONAL HERE

1. As you review the journal you've kept as you read this book, what has God been saying to you?
2. Each time you read this book, God will say new things to you because the Scriptures are alive and you will be in a different situation or phase. How can you keep these biblical truths alive for the future stirrings that God will bring?
3. How can you grow in the process of making disciples? (See Learning to Soar Discussion Guide for Small Groups.)
4. Who else needs to learn these lessons? How can you help them do so?

LEARNING TO SOAR DISCUSSION GUIDE FOR SMALL GROUPS

You will experience the most life change from applying *Learning to Soar* in a small-group process. This small-group guide provides step-by-step guidance to facilitate group study and discussion. If you would like more detail, an extended version of this guide is available at www.learningtosoar .org along with video clips that you can download.

This study employs an interactive learning process. Each group session can run anywhere from one to two hours depending on the choice of the group. Variable time increments for each segment of the session are suggested in this guide. Prior to each group meeting, members should read a chapter of the book and use a personal journal to process the questions at the end of the chapter.

BEFORE EACH SESSION

1. Read the chapter and answer the questions at the end of the chapter in your personal journal.
2. Pray for each member of your group.
3. Contact members of the group to see if you can help them grow through any transition or trial they are experiencing.
4. Prepare to show videos for the session. (See www.learningtosoar.org.)
5. For the first few meetings, prepare name tags for each member of the group or let them write on a blank name tag.
6. Prepare to tell the Bible story for the week in your own words and without notes. Don't try to memorize it. Practice telling the story as you see it unfold in your mind. (See the Guide to Bible Storytelling on the *Learning to Soar* website. Watch the video demonstration of Bible Storytelling.) After the first session or two, draft a volunteer to tell the following week's story. (This can be lively and fun!)

AFTER EACH SESSION

1. Jot down where you perceive each person to be on the Learning to Soar diagram (see page 20).
2. Plan to contact the group members by phone, e-mail, or in person. Ask questions and make yourself available to meet personally with people of your own sex or as couples.

3. Work with the volunteer as he or she prepares to tell the Bible story for that session. In the early sessions you will facilitate the group and lead the dialogue. As the group becomes more familiar with the procedure, you may ask them to lead the entire Bible story segment. The art of Bible Storytelling is taught on the website for you and the members to learn to communicate as Jesus did.
4. Pray each day about what God is saying to you and for each member of the group.

AFTER THE FINAL SESSION

1. Contact each of the members of the group and ask how you can pray for them or be of further help to them.
2. Ask if any will lead future *Learning to Soar* groups.
3. Offer to facilitate a discipleship group for those who are interested. Consider a proven, systematic developmental process such as one of the following:
   - The DESIGN FOR DISCIPLESHIP series by The Navigators (www.navpress.com)
   - The 2:7 series by The Navigators (www.navpress.com)
   - The LIFECHANGE series by The Navigators (www.navpress.com)
   - *MasterLife* by Avery T. Willis (www.lifeway.com)

If you enjoyed the Bible storytelling segments of this group study, you may want to consider the Bible Storying approach to discipleship demonstrated online at www.learningtosoar.org.

STIRRING THE NEST

Goal of the Session: To discover where God is working in our lives.

MY STORY — INTRODUCTION *(10–15 minutes)*

1. Ask each person to tell his or her name, what he or she does, and a little about each member of his or her family.
2. Ask each person to give one example of his or her nest being stirred and whom it affected.

GROUP REFLECTION — CHAPTER 1: STIRRING THE NEST *(10–15 minutes)*

Facilitate a discussion to answer the following questions. Watch for indications of where your group members might be on the Learning to Soar diagram so you can follow up and encourage them in their growth.

1. What idea struck you in this chapter? With whom did you identify?
2. What uncomfortable changes have you gone through recently that made you question God? Did you think at the time that God was involved in those changes?
3. Do you think God is stirring your nest now? In what ways? Why do you suppose He's doing this?

GOD'S STORY — EXODUS 1:6–2:25 *(30–45 minutes)*

Tell the group that you are going to share part of the Bible story that this chapter is based on and that you want them to listen and answer the following two questions:

1. Why were the people in trouble in Egypt?
2. Why do you think God allowed their nest to be stirred?

Tell in your own words the story from Exodus 1:6–2:25 of the Hebrews being enslaved and Moses' attempt to save them. After telling the story, ask questions using the outline below.

What? (Review)

Ask "what" questions about the story that will help group members remember the facts, the sequence, the main characters, and the dialogue.

So What? (Interpretation)

Now ask "why" questions about the story. Since the answers are open to interpretation, acknowledge any valid interpretation and follow it up if appropriate with other questions. Here are some sample questions:

- Why did the Egyptian leaders who had been so gracious to Joseph enslave the Hebrews?
- Why didn't God intervene and rescue them immediately?
- Why did Moses kill the Egyptian?
- Why did he run away to the desert?
- Why do you think God allowed this?

Now What? (Application)

Ask "how" questions about how they will apply what they have learned in the story and in the chapter. For example:

- What do you think God is telling you in this story about where you are with Him? How do you plan to respond?
- What do you think God is doing among His people in our day to stir their nests? How should we respond?
- What do you think God is telling our nation? How should we respond to this stirring?
- What are you personally going to do this week to apply what you have learned?

Your Story — Passing It On *(10–15 minutes)*

Ask each person to learn the story for the week, Exodus 1:6–2:25, and tell it to someone before the next session. They can tell the Bible story to a family member, friend, co-worker, or random acquaintance. If they can't find someone to listen, suggest they tell someone that they have an assignment from their small group to tell a story and then ask if they could tell it to him or her. They are free to ask (or not ask) the person questions about the story as the Spirit leads them.

Ask for a volunteer to tell the story to the group next week. Tell the volunteer that he or she should feel free to inject his or her personality into the storytelling (in other words, make it fun!) as long as the biblical details are told correctly. Assure the volunteer that you will introduce the story and lead the discussion. If no one volunteers to tell the story, say, "We will pass telling the Bible story to different group members each week, so begin learning how to do it and tell me when you are ready to take your turn." If necessary, tell the story yourself or privately enlist and train one of the group members to tell it.

Close in prayer.

IS THAT YOU, GOD?

Goal of the Session: To determine if God is stirring our nests and, if so, how and why.

MY STORY — INTRODUCTION *(10–15 minutes)*

1. Have several group members share their answer to one of the questions at the end of chapter 2.
2. Ask if anyone has a question they would like to ask the group.

GROUP REFLECTION — CHAPTER 2: IS THAT YOU, GOD? *(10–15 minutes)*

Ask volunteers to answer the following questions related to the chapter. Facilitate a discussion. Listen for indications of where they are on the Learning to Soar diagram so you can follow up with individuals during the week.

1. What stood out to you personally as you read chapter 2?
2. Is your nest being stirred? In what way? Who do you think is stirring your nest—God, Satan, or a particular person(s)? Why do you say that?
3. Do you think God would use the circumstances you are encountering *on purpose* to stir your nest and help you grow? If so, which of the items on page 40 under the heading "Understanding God's Stirrings" is He using? Is He using any other way?
4. What did you learn from Avery's two experiences about why God allowed those circumstances in his life? How do you respond to

his statement, "God is always getting you ready for your next assignment"?

God's Story — Exodus 3:1-22 (30–45 minutes)

Tell the group that the volunteer (or you) is going to tell the Bible story related to this chapter and you want them to listen and answer the following two questions:

1. Have you ever had a burning-bush experience? How was it like and unlike Moses' experience?
2. Why did God choose Moses to lead the Israelites out of slavery in Egypt?

Now have the volunteer tell in his or her own words the story of Moses' burning-bush experience in Exodus 3:1-22. After telling the story, ask questions using the outline below.

What? (Review)
Ask "what" questions about the details of the story to help group members remember the facts, the sequence, the main characters, and the dialogue.

So What? (Interpretation)
Pose "why" questions about the story. Since the answers are open to interpretation, acknowledge any valid interpretation and follow it up if appropriate with other questions. Here are some sample questions:

- Why did God choose to give Moses a burning-bush experience at this particular time?
- What do we learn about God in this story?
- What do you like about this story? What do you not like?
- How do you think you would have responded if you had been in Moses' sandals?

Now What? (Application)

Ask "how" questions about how they will apply what they have learned in the story and in the chapter. For example:

- What is God showing you about Himself?
- After seeing how God reveals Himself in this story, how do you think you should respond to what He is doing in your life now?
- What actions do you think you should take this week as a result of your current experience with God?
- What actions should we be taking as a small group this week to respond positively to God's work in our lives?

YOUR STORY — PASSING IT ON *(10–15 minutes)*

Ask each person to tell this week's story, Exodus 3:1-22, to someone else before the next group meeting and report to the group what happened. They can tell the Bible story to a family member, friend, co-worker, or random acquaintance.

Ask for a volunteer to tell next week's story about Israel crossing the Red Sea in Exodus 13:17–14:31. Assure them that you will set it up and lead the discussion afterward. If no one volunteers, try to enlist and train one of the group members privately during the week. (As a last resort, tell the story yourself.)

Close in prayer.

How Big Is Your God?

Goal of the Session: To be able to describe God's ability to solve any problem and to develop patience to wait until He does.

My Story — Introduction *(10–15 minutes)*

1. Ask volunteers to give examples of having to wait much longer than they anticipated for God to do something.
2. God hovered over for the Israelites when He caused ten plagues. How do you think He hovers over us today? Ask for personal examples.

Group Reflection — Chapter 3: How Big Is Your God? *(10–15 minutes)*

Pose the following questions related to the chapter and encourage discussion as group members provide answers.

1. If God gives you a command that you don't understand, what is your best course of action: Ignore it? Study it? Obey it? Why do you give that answer?
2. Think of an example from your own life of when you obeyed God but things didn't seem to turn out right. What did you do next? How can you have enough faith to do the next thing He tells you?
3. If you believe that God is big enough to handle all of your problems but a difficulty still exists in your life, why do you think God hasn't solved it yet?

GOD'S STORY — EXODUS 13:17–14:31 *(30–45 minutes)*

Ask the group to share their experiences of telling last week's story and the response they received.

Tell the group that because the story of the ten plagues is long, today's session will address the crossing of the Red Sea as the ultimate hovering over the Israelites. Introduce the volunteer who will be telling the story and instruct the group to think about the following questions as they listen:

1. Why didn't God lead the Israelites to cross the Red Sea immediately instead of leading them in a circle?
2. How well had the people of God learned the lesson of looking to Almighty God instead of their difficulties? Why do you say that?

Ask the volunteer to tell the story of crossing the Red Sea in his or her own words (see Exodus 13:17–14:31). After the story, ask questions using the outline below.

What? (Review)
Ask "what" questions about the story to help group members remember the facts, the sequence, the main characters, and the dialogue.

So What? (Interpretation)
Ask "why" questions about the story. Since the answers are open to interpretation, acknowledge any valid interpretation and follow it up if appropriate with other questions. Here are some sample questions:

- Why did they carry Joseph's bones with them?
- Why did God lure Pharaoh into chasing the Israelites?
- Why do you think the Israelites were terrified after they had seen the power of God in the ten plagues?
- How do you think the Israelites felt about God moving the pillar of cloud from in front of them to between them and Pharaoh's army?
- Why do you think God used Moses' staff to part and close the Red Sea?

- What do we learn about God in this story?
- What would have happened if they had not waited on God?

Now What? (Application)

Ask "how" questions about how group members will apply what they have learned in the story and in the chapter. For example:

- How does this story apply to our lives?
- What is God teaching you by leaving you in your circumstances even though He continues to demonstrate His power?
- What actions should you take as a result of experiencing this story?
- What do you think you should be telling other Christians who are complaining about their situations?

YOUR STORY — PASSING IT ON (10–15 minutes)

Ask each person to tell this week's story from Exodus 13:17–14:31 to someone before next week's group meeting and report back on how it was received. They can tell it to a family member, friend, co-worker, or random acquaintance.

Ask for a volunteer to tell the story for the coming week from Exodus 4:1-17. This is a short and easy story to tell. Tell them that you will set it up and facilitate the discussion afterward.

Close in prayer.

GROWING IN GOD'S WAYS

Goal of the Session: To understand that God's ways are not necessarily our ways.

MY STORY — INTRODUCTION *(10–15 minutes)*

1. Ask members to pair off and each share which of the five ways of God addressed in chapter 4 stood out to them for their personal spiritual journeys and why.
2. Instruct the pairs to tell one another how they can apply that way of God now.

GROUP REFLECTION — CHAPTER 4: GROWING IN GOD'S WAYS *(10–15 minutes)*

After you assemble back together, facilitate a discussion of this week's chapter using the sample questions below. Listen for indications of where group members are on the Learning to Soar diagram so you can pray for and encourage them during the week.

1. Which of the five ways of God mentioned in this chapter is most imperative for you to learn in order to respond to God's hovering? Why?
2. How can you apply that way of God now?
3. Why do you think God prepares *individuals* to lead before He leads His entire people?

4. What ordinary things has God used in your life to do extraordinary things?
5. What ordinary things in your life have you not given to God because you thought they were too ordinary?
6. Share about a time when God asked you to do something that did not make sense to you at first. What did you ultimately learn from this experience?
7. Tell about a difficult thing God allowed to happen to you even after you obeyed. How did you respond and what did you learn from the experience?

GOD'S STORY — EXODUS 4:1-17 (30–45 minutes)

Introduce the person who will be telling the story from Exodus 4:1-17 and ask group members to listen for the answers to the following questions:

1. How did God answer Moses' objections?
2. What happens when you obey God's call? When you disobey it?

What? (Review)
Ask "what" questions about the story that will help the group remember the facts, the sequence of events, the main characters, and the dialogue.

So What? (Interpretation)
Ask "why" questions about the story:

- Why do you think Moses was so reluctant to do what God asked of him?
- Why do you think God was so patient with Moses' objections?
- Why was God angry with Moses?
- Why does God sometimes give us second best?
- What do we learn about humans in this story?
- What do we learn about God in this story?
- How do you think Moses' life would have been different if he had fully believed and obeyed God?

Now What? (Application)

Ask "how" questions about how group members can apply what they have learned in the story and in the chapter. For example:

- If God gives you a command that you don't understand, what is your best course of action? Why?
- What would it take for you to believe and obey God when He tells you what to do?
- What's likely to happen if you fail to believe and obey God?
- How can you apply this story to your personal walk with God?

YOUR STORY — PASSING IT ON *(10–15 minutes)*

Ask each person to tell this week's story from Exodus 4:1-17 to someone before next week's meeting and report to the group how it was received.

Ask for a volunteer to tell the story of how Israel failed to enter the Promised Land (Numbers 13:26–14:25) at next week's meeting. (Avoid having the same person tell the stories from week to week; it is better if everyone is given a chance to tell one of the Bible stories. Encourage them to put their own personalities into it and offer to give them whatever help they may need to prepare to tell it.)

Close in prayer.

TRY, TRY AGAIN

Goal of the Session: To be willing to take the risk of faith to do whatever God asks.

MY STORY — INTRODUCTION *(10–15 minutes)*

1. Ask the group to tell what happened when they told last week's story to someone.
2. Ask members to share an experience of when they took a risk based on faith.

GROUP REFLECTION — CHAPTER 5: TRY, TRY AGAIN *(10–15 minutes)*

Facilitate a discussion of this week's chapter using the following questions:

1. What stood out to you most from this chapter? Why?
2. How does an eagle learn to fly?
3. What kinds of situations did God put Israel in again and again that required them to risk by faith?
4. What kinds of situations has God put you in that required you to risk by faith?
5. Why do you think God tested the Israelites (see Deuteronomy 8:2-5)? Can you think of a time when God may have tested you for the same reasons?
6. What is the value of trying and failing in the Christian life?

GOD'S STORY — NUMBERS 13:26–14:25
(30–45 minutes)

Introduce the person who is to tell the story from Numbers 13:26–14:25 and ask the group members to watch for the answers to the following questions as they listen:

1. Why did the Israelites not enter the Promised Land when God told them to?
2. What was the result for the adult Israelites? For Joshua and Caleb?

What? (Review)
Ask "what" questions about the story to review the facts, the sequence of events, the main characters, and the dialogue.

So What? (Interpretation)
Ask questions that will underscore the "why" of the story:

- After seeing so many miracles of God in Egypt and then in the desert for eighteen months, why do you think the Israelites refused to enter the Promised Land when God told them to?
- Why do you think they grumbled at Moses and God for bringing them to this point?
- Why do you think Joshua and Caleb gave a different report and urged the people to take the land?
- Why did Moses plead with God not to destroy the Israelites?
- Why do you think God listened to Moses and changed the plan?
- Why do you think Israel failed when they did try to take the land?
- What does this story underscore about the relationship between risk and faith?

Now What? (Application)
Ask "how" questions to help the group apply what they learned in the story and in the chapter. For example:

- Think of a situation you're now facing. How can you apply what we've learned from this session?
- How can you encourage each other to obey God the first time?
- How can you use this story and this chapter to counsel a person who has failed?

YOUR STORY — PASSING IT ON *(10–15 minutes)*

Ask each person to tell this week's story (Numbers 13:26–14:25) to someone during the week and report how it was received.

Ask for a volunteer to serve as storyteller at next week's meeting (Joshua 14:6-14).

Close in prayer.

GROWING YOUR FAITH THROUGH A WORD FROM GOD

Goal of the Session: To be able to explain how to receive a word from God, verify its application to their situation, and act on it.

MY STORY — INTRODUCTION *(10–15 minutes)*

1. Ask members to pair off and do two things:
   - Share what happened when they told last week's story to someone.
   - Share something they have written in their journals as they read the book. (If they haven't written anything, have them share an insight from this week's chapter that caught their attention and why it stood out to them.)
2. Call the group back together and ask members to share an experience of getting a word from God and seeing God answer that promise.

GROUP REFLECTION — CHAPTER 6: GROWING YOUR FAITH THROUGH A WORD FROM GOD
(10–15 minutes)

Facilitate a discussion of this week's chapter using the following questions:

1. What do you think a word from God is? Do you agree or disagree

that God directs you to specific passages of Scripture to apply to
your life? Why or why not?

2. What is an example of how people might misuse this approach?
3. What are the six steps in building a dynamic faith through getting a
   word from God?
4. How can you test whether you truly have a word from God for a
   specific situation?
5. What role do circumstances play in discerning a word from God?
   How can you test the circumstances to see if they line up with God's
   purpose and your spiritual markers?
6. Can you trust the counsel of other Christians? Explain why or why
   not.
7. How has God grown your faith through applying specific verses or
   passages from the Bible to a situation in your life?

GOD'S STORY — JOSHUA 14:6-14 *(30–45 minutes)*

Introduce the person who is to tell the story from Joshua 14:6-14 and ask
group members to look for the answers to the following questions as they
listen:

1. On what did Caleb base his faith?
2. What effect did God's promise have on Caleb's life?

After telling the story, ask questions following the outline below.

What? (Review)
Ask "what" questions about the story to review the facts, the sequence of
events, the main characters, and the dialogue.

So What? (Interpretation)
Ask "why" questions about the story using the following questions:

- Why do you think God allowed Caleb and Joshua to conquer the
  Promised Land?

- What one word described how Caleb followed God? [whole-heartedly] Why do you think this word was used?
- Why do you think Caleb was as strong and vigorous to go into battle at age eighty-five as he was when he received the promise from God forty-five years earlier?
- Why do you think Caleb asked for the land inhabited by the giants?
- What do we learn about God's promises in this story?
- What do we learn about our response to God's promises?

Now What? (Application)

Ask "how" questions about how group members will apply what they have learned in the story and in the chapter. For example:

- What is God challenging you to believe now as the next step in building your faith? What do you think God wants you to do about it?
- From our study so far (this session or previous sessions), is there a particular scripture you feel God wants to apply to your personal life? Why?
- How will you apply these lessons to your life this week?

YOUR STORY — PASSING IT ON (10–15 minutes)

Ask each person to tell this week's story of Caleb from Joshua 14:6-14 to someone before the next group meeting and report how it was received.

Ask for a volunteer to tell the story to the group in next week's meeting (Joshua 3–4). Offer whatever help he or she may need to prepare to tell it.

Close in prayer.

THE POWER OF HIS SPIRIT

Goal of the Session: To be able to explain how to be filled with the Spirit and depend on God to do His work through you.

MY STORY — INTRODUCTION *(10–15 minutes)*

Ask members to share an experience of when they tried to do something for God in their own power (not God's). How did it turn out, and what did they learn from the experience?

GROUP REFLECTION — CHAPTER 7: THE POWER OF HIS SPIRIT *(10–15 minutes)*

Facilitate a discussion of this week's chapter using the following questions. Continue to listen for indications of where group members are on the Learning to Soar diagram so you can pray for them and follow up personally.

1. How do eagles soar? What's the difference between flying and soaring?
2. How is the Holy Spirit in the life of the Christian similar to the wind under the eagle's wings?
3. What does it mean to be filled with the Spirit?
4. How is one filled with the Spirit?

5. In what new ways can you allow God's Spirit and power to flow through you?

6. What role do God's overall purposes have in one's soaring?

7. Consider the author's statement, "Success is best measured by the difference between what you can do alone compared to what God can do through you." Do you agree or disagree? Why?

8. What does the prayer of Jabez (see 1 Chronicles 4:9-10) challenge you to do? How much of God's potential do you think you have experienced?

GOD'S STORY — JOSHUA 3–4 (30–45 minutes)

Introduce the person who is to tell the story from Joshua 3–4 and encourage group members to look for the answers to the following questions as they listen:

1. When did Joshua exercise faith? When did the priests exercise faith? When did the people exercise faith?

2. How was crossing the Jordan like an eagle's soaring?

What? (Review)
Following the story, ask "what" questions to review the facts, the sequence of events, the main characters, and the dialogue.

So What? (Interpretation)
Ask "why" questions about the story using the following questions:

• Why did God ask the Israelites to consecrate themselves for three days?

• Why do you think God gave the promise that the Jordan would stop flowing? What is the relationship between God's promises and our obedience?

• What do you learn about God's promises in this story?

• What do you learn about our response to God's promises?

Now What? (Application)

Ask "how" questions about how group members will apply what they've learned from the story and the chapter. For example:

- Can you think of a specific step of faith in your life that was like the Israelites' act of stepping into the swollen Jordan River?
- What have you learned from this week's chapter that you think will help you move forward in God's power this week?
- How can we pray for you? (Spend time praying for the requests.)

YOUR STORY — PASSING IT ON *(10–15 minutes)*

Ask each person to tell this week's story of Joshua from Joshua 3–4 to someone before the next group meeting and report how it was received.

Ask for *two* volunteers to tell two new stories to the group at next week's meeting.

- One will tell the story of conquering Jericho from Joshua 6.
- The other will tell the story of Ai from Joshua 7–8. (He or she will not tell all the details, just the main story.)

Offer to give them whatever help they need to prepare to tell it.

Ask for personal prayer requests and close in prayer. (Be sure everyone's requests are prayed for.)

SOAR ABOVE THE STORMS AND EPILOGUE

Goal of the Session: To know how God prepares us to rise above life's storms and soar with Him.

MY STORY — INTRODUCTION *(10–15 minutes)*

Ask members one by one to share where they think they were on the Learning to Soar diagram (see page 20) when they started the study, where they are now, what their plans are to continue to grow, and what level they plan to achieve in the future.

Ask several members of the group to volunteer to say a brief prayer for each person as they share.

GROUP REFLECTION — CHAPTER 8: SOAR ABOVE THE STORMS AND EPILOGUE *(10–15 minutes)*

Using the following questions, facilitate a discussion of this week's chapter and epilogue:

1. Why is learning to soar not optional for eagles? Why is it not optional for disciples?
2. How do eagles use storms for their benefit? How should Christians use trials for their benefit?
3. What is God's perspective on the storms in your life?

4. What vision do you feel God may be asking you to work on that can't be completed in your lifetime?
5. What might God be prompting you to do to prepare others to complete the vision He is giving you?
6. Have any of you had a mentor? Are you mentoring anyone?
7. What is a mentor's role in discipling others?
8. What are you going to do to continue to grow as a disciple? (Refer to the recommended resources in the appendix on page 173.) Ask them if they would like to consider continuing this small group or adding others to it for future studies.

GOD'S STORY — JOSHUA 6–8 *(30–45 minutes)*

Introduce the people who will tell the stories from Joshua 6 and Joshua 7–8. Explain that we are using two stories because they vividly contrast doing things in our own power and doing them in God's power—and learning to soar above the storms as Joshua did.

For the story from Joshua 6, encourage group members to listen for answers to the following two questions:

1. Why did God command the Israelites to conquer Jericho in the way He did?
2. What was the role of God's people before the wall fell and afterward?

Prior to the telling of the story of Ai from Joshua 7–8, encourage the group to listen for answers to these two questions:

1. Why were the Israelites defeated at Ai?
2. What different strategy did God use to conquer Ai?

What? (Review)
Ask "what" questions about the stories that will help review the facts, the sequence of events, the main characters, and the dialogue.

So What? (Interpretation)

Ask "why" questions about the story using the following sample questions:

- Why did God ask the people to walk around and blow trumpets before the wall fell down and then to fight and destroy everything after the wall fell?
- Why did God tell them to destroy everything in Jericho?
- Why do you think God allowed the entire people to be defeated for one person's sin?
- How do an individual's sins affect God's whole people?
- Why did God use a different strategy to conquer Ai?
- Why did Joshua read all the laws of Moses to the people at Mount Ebal and Mount Gerizim?
- What is the difference between the way you respond to a storm that you caused (like Achan at Jericho) and one that you did not cause (like Joshua in the same situation)?

Now What? (Application)

Ask "how" questions about how they will apply what they have learned in the story and in the chapter. For example:

- Where are you in the stirring to soaring process? What potential do you believe God has created within you?
- What is God prompting you to do that doesn't seem like common sense but will cause you to depend on Him?
- What steps will you take to overcome the sins and obstacles that prevent you from being used by God?
- What is the number one thing God is asking you to do as a result of this study?

YOUR STORY — PASSING IT ON (10–15 minutes)

Challenge the group to share with someone this week what they've learned from this study of the eagle's development: how it parallels the story of the Israelites and how it serves as a metaphor for an individual's personal spiritual growth, maturity, and mission. Ask them to tell one or both of the stories (Joshua 6–8) to someone this week.

Close in prayer for each other.

RECOMMENDED RESOURCES

FURTHER DISCIPLESHIP

MasterLife: A Biblical Process for Growing Disciples by Avery T. Willis Jr. with Kay Moore (www.lifeway.org). All the *MasterLife* resources are available from www.lifeway.org, www.averywillis.org, www.learningtosoar.org, and www.amazon.com.

- *MasterLife 1: The Disciple's Cross*
- *MasterLife 2: The Disciple's Personality*
- *MasterLife 3: The Disciple's Victory*
- *MasterLife 4: The Disciple's Mission*
- *The MasterLife Book Set* contains all four *MasterLife* Member Books above (four books of six-week sessions each) in a slipcase at a savings.
- *The MasterLife Leader's Kit* includes a detailed leader's guide and three DVDs.
- *MasterLife: Developing a Rich Personal Relationship with the Master* by Avery T. Willis Jr. and Sherrie Willis Brown — a paperback book of the content without the discipleship process. It gives the leader or small-group member an overview of the *MasterLife* content but is not a substitute for the small-group discipling process.

Design for Discipleship Series by The Navigators (www.navpress.com)

- *Design for Discipleship 1: Your Life in Christ*
- *Design for Discipleship 2: The Spirit-Filled Christian*
- *Design for Discipleship 3: Walking with Christ*
- *Design for Discipleship 4: The Character of the Christian*
- *Design for Discipleship 5: Foundations for Faith*
- *Design for Discipleship 6: Growing in Discipleship*
- *Design for Discipleship 7: Our Hope in Christ*

2:7 Series by The Navigators (www.navpress.com)

- *Growing Strong in God's Family*
- *Deepening Your Roots in God's Family*
- *Bearing Fruit in God's Family*

LifeChange Series — group studies of individual books of the Bible by NavPress (www.navpress.com)

Missions

The Biblical Basis of Missions: Your Mission as a Christian by Avery T. Willis Jr. (Convention Press)
This book is available only by download at www.averywillis.org or www .imb.org.

On Mission with God: Living God's Purpose for His Glory by Avery T. Willis Jr. and Henry T. Blackaby (LifeWay Christian Resources)
A natural follow-up for *Experiencing God* by Henry Blackaby and *MasterLife* by Avery Willis, this book uses the stories of the Bible's seven key characters (Abraham, Moses, David, Jesus, Peter, Paul, and John) to show how God involves us in His mission for His glory. The following resources are for use in an eight-week small-group study.

- *On Mission with God* workbook
- *On Mission with God* leader's kit with videos for each session
- *On Mission with God* hardback book

These resources are available from www.averywillis.org, www .learningtosoar.org, www.lifeway.com, and www.amazon.com. The hardback book is available only from www.averywillis.org.

On Mission with God, a module of seven audio CDs telling eighty-eight Bible stories from the lives of the seven characters featured in the book above. It is Module 7 in the FOLLOWING JESUS: MAKING DISCIPLES OF ORAL LEARNERS series by Avery T. Willis Jr. et al. Available from www .learningtosoar.org, www.imb.org, and www.fjseries.org.

ORALITY

Your church can start a Bible Storying project:

- In an unreached people group — visit www.finishingthetask.com
- In the United States — visit www.reallifeministries.com/leaders
- With youth — visit www.echothestory.com

How to do Bible Storying: www.chronologicalbiblestorying.com

Free download of the book *Making Disciples of Oral Learners*, which introduces orality:

- www.internationaloralitynetwork.com
- www.OralStrategies.com
- www.learningtosoar.org

Purchase the interactive course *Tell the Story: A Primer on Chronological Bible Storying*: www.imbresources.org

Orality Ministries:

- www.averywillis.org
- www.OneStory.org
- www.go2southasia.org

- www.gods-story.org/sts
- www.siutraining.org
- www.storyrunners.com
- www.wycliffeonestory.info
- www.ywamonestory.org

Books:
Making Disciples of Oral Learners can be purchased at www.imbresources .org or downloaded free at www.oralbible.com. Available in English, Chinese traditional and simplified script, Spanish, and Portuguese. Audio book also available. The book has an extensive bibliography of secular and religious books, resources, and organizations related to orality.

The Art of Storytelling by John Walsh. Chicago: Moody, 2003.

Basic Bible Storying by Dr. J. O. Terry. Fort Worth, TX: Church Starting Network, 2007. www.churchstarting.net/books.htm

Shaped by the Story by Michael Novelli. Grand Rapids, MI: Zondervan, 2008.

VIDEOS

Telling the Story DVD — Introduction to orality with examples. www.imb .org

Orality Around the World DVD — Fourteen vignettes of storying around the world. www.imb.org

This list is intended to be brief. There are many more good resources available on the websites listed above.

ORGANIZATIONS (IN WHICH AVERY HAS A LEADERSHIP ROLE)

International Orality Network is a network of more than one hundred organizations making God's Word available to oral learners in culturally appropriate ways that enable church-planting movements everywhere. www.oralbible.com

Call2All is a worldwide, strategy-centered, and action-oriented movement calling the church to a renewed, focused collaborative effort to complete the Great Commission. It convenes Christian leaders in strategy congresses and provides new avenues for training in comprehensive strategies in orality, church planting, evangelism, prayer, unreached people groups, geographical mapping, and compassion ministries to reach the last, the least, and the lost. www.call2all.org

Finishing the Task is a global network of local churches, denominations, church planters, and missions agencies that are working together in partnership to see church-planting initiatives launched initially among the 639 unengaged, unreached people groups of the world with populations over 100,000 and eventually all people groups. www.finishingthetask.org

Avery T. Willis Center for Global Outreach at Oklahoma Baptist University, Shawnee, Oklahoma, equips students for vocational Christian service any place on the globe, provides missiological research tools for students engaged in the study of missions, and prepares them for short-term volunteer assignments. It helps students, faculty, and staff to develop and live out a missions lifestyle through hosting missions conferences, developing missions education resources, and coordinating short-term opportunities for mission service in our nation and throughout the world. www.okbu.edu/go

Real Life Ministries Church, Post Falls, Idaho, is a church where Avery has taught them to use Bible Storying in their small groups to reach seven thousand people. He has taught them this model through the Real Life

Partnership model, and he is committed to helping other churches use this same model. See *Church Is a Team Sport* by Jim Putman (Baker, 2008). www.reallifeministries.com

Trans World Radio is the most far-reaching Christian radio network in the world. Programs in more than 225 languages and dialects are aired from more than 2,000 outlets. Every day their broadcasts reach millions in more than 160 countries. Avery serves on its board of directors. www.twr.org

Notes

Chapter 1: Stirring the Nest

1. Lea MacNally, *The Ways of an Eagle* (London: Collins and Harvill, 1977), 41–42.
2. Laura Erickson, "About Bald Eagle Nests," *Journey North* © 2008, www.learner.org/jnorth/tm/eagle/NestAbout1.html (accessed December 19, 2008).
3. Peter Nye, "About Bald Eagle Nests," *Journey North* © 2008, www .learner.org/jnorth/tm/eagle/NestAbout.html (accessed December 18, 2008).
4. Johanna Johnston, *The Eagle in Fact and Fiction* (New York: Harlin Quest, 1966), 27.
5. Jana McConoughey, *The Bald Eagle* (Mankato, MN: Crestwood House, 1983), 22.
6. Spiros Zodhiates, Warren Baker, and Joel Kletzing, eds., "Hebrew and Chaldee Dictionary," *Hebrew-Greek Key Word Study Bible: New American Standard Bible*, rev. ed. (Chattanooga, TN: AMG International, 2008), 86.
7. R. A. Torrey, DD, *Why God Used D. L. Moody* (New York: Revell, 1923), www.mun.ca/rels/restmov/texts/dasc/WGUDLM.THM.

Chapter 2: Is That You, God?

1. Herbert Lockyer Sr., ed., *Illustrated Dictionary of the Bible* (Nashville: Thomas Nelson, 1986), 1062.
2. Avery Willis with Sherrie Willis Brown, *MasterLife: Developing a Rich Personal Relationship with the Master* (Nashville: Broadman & Holman, 1998).
3. David Livingstone, in a speech given at Cambridge in 1857, transcribed at "David Livingstone," The Cooper Union, Humanities and Social Sciences Department, www.cooper.edu/humanities/classes/coreclasses/hss3/d_livingstone.html (accessed December 18, 2008).

CHAPTER 3: HOW BIG IS YOUR GOD?

1. Joe Van Wormer, *Eagles* (New York: E. P. Dutton, 1985), 1.

2. Andy Stanley, quoted in Bruce Wilkinson, *The Vision of the Leader* (Atlanta: WorldTeach, 2000).

3. Lea MacNally, *The Ways of an Eagle* (London: Collins and Harvill, 1977), 37; see also David H. Ellis, "Development of Behavior in the Golden Eagle," *The Journal of Wildlife Management*, October 1979.

4. *The Family Circus*, Bil Keane, Inc., June 10, 2005.

5. "Ask Us—Aircraft Speed Records," Aerospaceweb.org © 1997–2008, www.aerospaceweb.org/question/performance/q0023.shtml (accessed December 20, 2008). That's 17,000 mph for the fastest winged, manned vehicle.

6. "How Long Does It Take to Get to the Moon?" *Discovery* 2001, www.discoverymagazine.com/digger/d98dd/d9807dd.html (accessed December 20, 2008).

7. James Woods, "Light Speed, an Alternative Theory," *The American Chronicle*, July 1, 2008, www.americanchronicle.com/articles/66894 (accessed December 20, 2008).

8. Terence Dickinson, *Exploring the Night Sky: The Equinox Astronomy Guide for Beginners* (Ontario: Firefly Books, 1997), 26.

9. "Cosmic Distance Scales—The Nearest Star," Astrophysics Science Division, NASA/Goddard Space Flight Center, http://heasarc.gsfc .nasa.gov/docs/cosmic/nearest_star_info.html (accessed December 20, 2008).

10. "The Closest Star," Hyperphysics-Physics/Astonomy Department, Georgia State University, http://hyperphysics.phy-astr.gsu.edu/hbase/ starlog/strclos.html (accessed December 20, 2008).

11. "Ask Us—Interstellar Spacecraft," Aerospaceweb.org © 1997–2008, www.aerospaceweb.org/question/spacecraft/q0225.shtml (accessed December 20, 2008).

12. "Home Page," *Enchanted Learning* © 1996–2007, www .enchantedlearning.com (accessed January 15, 2005).

13. Dickinson, 21; see also *Sky News*, www.skynewsmagazine.com.

14. "Andromeda Galaxy," Sol Company, www.solstation.com/x-objects/ andromeda.htm (accessed February 7, 2009).

15. "The Local Group of Galaxies," Students for the Exploration and Development of Space, www.seds.org/messier/more/local.html (accessed February 7, 2009).

16. "The Local Group of Galaxies" (accessed December 20, 2008). The Local Group has a diameter of ten million light-years.
17. Ian O'Neill, "13.73 Billion Years—The Most Precise Measurement of the Age of the Universe Yet," *Universe Today,* March 28, 2008, www.universetoday.com/2008/03/28/1373-billion-years-the-most-accurate-measurement-of-the-age-of-the-universe-yet (accessed February 7, 2009).
18. Frikkie de Bruyn, "The Mass of the Universe," The Astronomical Society of Southern Africa, www.saao.ac.za/assa/features/cosmology-articles/mass-of-the-universe.doc (accessed February 7, 2009).
19. "Ask a Scientist," Argonne National Laboratory: Division of Educational Programs, U.S. Department of Energy, www.newton.dep.anl.gov/askasci/ast99/ast99215.htm (accessed December 3, 2008).
20. Author's transcription of a message preached (and recorded) at the Global Pastors Network Billion Soul Pastors Conference in Orlando, Florida, January 2006.

Chapter 4: Growing in God's Ways

1. Matthew Henry, *Matthew Henry's Commentary on the Old Testament* (Electronic Edition STEP Files, QuickVerse, 2005), verses 8-16.
2. John Piper, in a speech given to the Passion Conference on January 2, 1997, available online at www.desiringgod.org/ResourceLibrary/ConferenceMessages/ByDate/1997/1906_Passion_for_the_Supremacy_of_God_Part_1 (accessed December 3, 2008).
3. William Booth, quoted in *It's My Turn* (Denver: Kingdom Building Ministries, 1996), 76–77.
4. *It's My Turn,* 11.
5. Wade Akins, *Be a 24/7 Christian* (Garland, TX: Hannibal Books, 2005), 164–167.

Chapter 5: Try, Try Again

1. Lea MacNally, *The Ways of an Eagle* (London: Collins and Harvill, 1977), 50.
2. MacNally, 51.
3. *What About Bob?,* directed by Frank Oz (Burbank, CA: Touchstone Pictures, 1991).

4. David H. Ellis, "Development of Behavior in the Golden Eagle," *The Journal of Wildlife Management,* October 1979.
5. Ellis.
6. Jana McConoughey, *The Bald Eagle* (Mankato, MN: Crestwood House, 1983), 22.
7. Mark V. Stalmaster, *The Bald Eagle* (New York: Universe Books, 1987), 77–78.
8. Arthur Cleveland Bent, *Life Histories of North American Birds of Prey,* part I (Washington, D.C.: Smithsonian Institution United States National Museum, Bulletin *167,* United States Government Printing Office, 1937), 302, quoted in Frederic R. Howe and George F. Howe, "Moses and the Eagle," *Journal of the American Scientific Affiliation* 20 (March 1968): 22–24, www.asa3.org/ASA/PSCF/1968/JASA3 -68Howe.html (accessed December 20, 2008).
9. Frances Hamerstrom, *An Eagle to the Sky* (Ames, IA: Iowa State University Press, 1970), xix–xx. Also available at Sandy Warner, "To Fly Like an Eagle," www.prophetic.net/eagles.htm (accessed December 20, 2008).
10. Rick Brekelbaum, interview with the author, October 1, 2008.
11. Laurie Campbell and Roy Dennis, *Golden Eagles* (Grantown-on-Spey, Scotland: Colin Baxter, 1996), 65.
12. Stalmaster, 78.
13. Ellis.
14. Jon M. Gerrard and Gary R. Bortolotti, *The Bald Eagle: Haunts and Habits of a Wilderness Monarch* (Washington, D.C.: Smithsonian Institution Press, 1988), 98–99.
15. Joe Van Wormer, *Eagles* (New York: E. P. Dutton, 1985), 37.
16. Ellis.
17. Bruce Wilkinson, *The Vision of the Leader* (Atlanta: WorldTeach, 2000), 45.
18. Wilkinson, 63.
19. "Bald Eagles," DverCity © 1999–2008, www.Dvercity.com/bald _eagles.html (accessed December 20, 2008).
20. MacNally, 122–123.
21. Herbert Lockyer Sr., ed., *Illustrated Dictionary of the Bible* (Nashville: Thomas Nelson, 1986), 519.
22. Van Wormer, 9.
23. Campbell and Dennis, 65.

24. Candace Savage, *Eagles of North America* (Vancouver: Greystone Books, 1987), 107.
25. Johanna Johnston, *The Eagle in Fact and Fiction* (New York: Harlin Quest, 1966), 36.

CHAPTER 6: GROWING YOUR FAITH THROUGH A WORD FROM GOD

1. Joe McKeever, "Does God Answer Prayer? Monica Knows," *Baptist Press*, August 6, 2002, www.bpnews.net/bpnews.asp?ID=13976.

CHAPTER 7: THE POWER OF HIS SPIRIT

1. "Bald Eagle Fact Sheet: Natural History, Ecology, and History of Recovery," U.S. Fish and Wildlife Service, www.fws.gov/midwest/ eagle/recovery/biologue.html (accessed December 22, 2008).
2. Jon M. Gerrard and Gary R. Bortolotti, *The Bald Eagle: Haunts and Habits of a Wilderness Monarch* (Washington, D.C.: Smithsonian Institution Press, 1988), 24.
3. Avery T. Willis Jr., *The Biblical Basis of Missions* (Nashville: Baptist Sunday School Board, 1992), 63–64.
4. Gerrard and Bortolotti, 107.
5. Henry Blackaby and Richard Blackaby, *Called to be God's Leader* (Nashville: Thomas Nelson, 2004), 129.
6. For more information on these organizations, see the appendix on page 173.
7. "Karen Bennett," Andy Stanley, www.rightnow.org/contentDetail .aspx?id=1104&sid=1001 (accessed January 15, 2005). Derived from Andy Stanley, *Visioneering* (Sisters, OR: Multnomah, 1999), 129–131.
8. Bruce Wilkinson, *The Vision of the Leader* (Atlanta: WorldTeach, 2000), 59.

CHAPTER 8: SOAR ABOVE THE STORMS

1. Candace Savage, *Eagles of North America* (Vancouver: Greystone Books, 1987), 13.
2. Nigel Risner, "Breaking Down the Barriers in Your Mind," *A Career in Your Suitcase*, career.cabalgroup.com/Articles/MIH/barriers.htm (accessed December 3, 2008).
3. "Eagle," U.S. Army Corps of Engineers (St. Louis District), www.mvs .usace.army.mil/Rivers/eagle.html (accessed January 15, 2005).

4. Hope Rutledge, "A Bald Eagle's Eyesight and Hearing," Baldeagleinfo .com © 1999–2008, www.baldeagleinfo.com/eagle/eagle2.html (accessed December 22, 2008).

5. Jana McConoughey, *The Bald Eagle* (Mankato, MN: Crestwood House, 1983), 9.

6. "Eagle," U.S. Army Corps of Engineers.

7. Peter Nye, "Frequently Asked Questions," *Journey North* © 2008, www.learner.org/jnorth/www/critters/eagle/826572782.html (accessed December 22, 2008).

8. Lea MacNally, *The Ways of an Eagle* (London: Collins and Harvill, 1977), 31.

9. "Mount Rushmore Information," *SD Web Traveler*, www .mountrushmoreinfo.com.

10. "Honoring the 60th Anniversary of the Commencement of the Carving of the Crazy Horse Memorial," Congressional record, section 17, May 19, 2008, http://www.govtrack.us/congress/record .xpd?id=110-h20080519-17.

11. Margaret Odrowaz-Sypniewska, "One Polish-American's Dream Continues—Twenty-Five Years After His Death (in 2007)," www .angelfire.com/mi4/polcrt/KZiolkowski.html.

12. "Crazy Horse Memorial Research," HighBeam Research, www .encyclopedia.com/topic/Crazy_Horse_Memorial.aspx.

13. Jon M. Gerrard and Gary R. Bortolotti, *The Bald Eagle: Haunts and Habits of a Wilderness Monarch* (Washington, D.C.: Smithsonian Institution Press, 1988), 24.

14. You can read a transcript of it online at christianelibrary.googlepages .com/btr_dawson.html.

15. Dawson Trotman, *Born to Reproduce* (Lincoln, NE: Back to the Bible, undated), 34.

16. See Avery's website at www.averywillis.org and the appendix on page 173.

17. "Salinity," Amazines © 2008, www.amazines.com/Salinity_related. html (accessed December 3, 2008).

Epilogue

1. Now Marcia Tapp Stutes.

ABOUT THE
AUTHORS

AVERY T. WILLIS JR. is an international author, leader, speaker, and conference leader. Among other things, he serves as executive director of the International Orality Network and ambassador-at-large for the Avery T. Willis Center for Global Outreach at Oklahoma Baptist University.

He was a pastor for ten years before serving with his wife, Shirley, and their five children as missionaries in Indonesia for fourteen years. He may be best known for creating the *MasterLife* discipleship materials in Indonesia while serving as the president of the Indonesian Baptist Theological Seminary. They have been translated into more than fifty languages and are used in more than one hundred countries. Avery led the adult discipleship department for LifeWay Christian Resources, providing discipleship and family resources, for fifteen years. He then served for ten years as senior vice president for overseas operations of the Southern Baptist Convention's International Mission Board, overseeing the work of 5,600 missionaries in 183 countries.

Avery holds a BA degree from Oklahoma Baptist University and a MDiv and ThD degree from Southwestern Baptist Theological Seminary. He has received honorary doctoral degrees from Oklahoma Baptist University and Southwest Baptist University. His writings include *MasterLife: Discipleship Training* and *MasterBuilder: Multiplying Leaders*; he is also associate editor of the *Disciple's Study Bible* and coauthor of *On Mission with God*; *Following Jesus: Making Disciples of Oral Learners*; *Lead Like Jesus*; and many other books.

He and his wife currently live in Arkansas. The loves of their lives are their five children and sixteen grandchildren, who are dynamic Christians, plus two young great-grandchildren.

MATT WILLIS is currently ministering in south Asia. He has served as the coordinator of the Avery T. Willis Center for Global Outreach at Oklahoma Baptist University, the English minister at Oklahoma City Chinese Baptist Church, and with International Students Inc. at Texas Christian University.

Matt is the oldest grandchild of Avery Willis. He and his wife, Allison, have two children. He holds a BA degree in communication studies from Oklahoma Baptist University in Shawnee, Oklahoma, and a Master of Divinity from Southwestern Baptist Theological Seminary in Fort Worth, Texas.

Correspondence
Avery Willis
www.averywillis.org
avery@averywillis.org
www.learningtosoar.org

Matt Willis
82willis@gmail.com
www.learningtosoar.org

More great titles from NavPress!

Respectable Sins

Jerry Bridges

978-1-60006-140-0

Are some sins acceptable? It seems we have created a sliding scale where gossip, jealousy, and selfishness comfortably exist within the church. Acclaimed author Jerry Bridges believes that just as culture has lost the concept of sin, the church faces the same danger. Drawing from scriptural truth, he sheds light on subtle behaviors that can derail our spiritual growth.

Souvenirs of Solitude

Brennan Manning

978-1-60006-867-6

The most reliable guides of spiritual formation pinpoint solitude and silence as central to the spiritual life. Now Brennan Manning—in his honest, original, and winning way—shares from his own experiences to prompt the reader into the riches of spending time alone with God.

Christian Coaching, Second Edition

Gary R. Collins, PhD

978-1-60006-361-9

Dr. Gary R. Collins takes the successful principles of coaching and gives them a God-centered application. Broader in scope than either mentoring or discipling, Christian coaching helps people find God's vision for their lives and learn to live accordingly.

To order copies, call NavPress at 1-800-366-7788 or log on to
www.navpress.com.

.